THE VISION THAT CHANGED A NATION

The Legacy of
William Tennent

JOHN F.

MorningStar Publications
A DIVISION OF MORNINGSTAR FELLOWSHIP CHURCH
375 Star Light Drive, Fort Mill, SC 29715

The Vision That Changed a Nation: The Legacy of William Tennent
Copyright © 2007 by John F. Hansen

Distributed by MorningStar Publications, Inc., a division of MorningStar
Fellowship Church, 375 Star Light Drive, Fort Mill, SC 29715

International Standard Book Number: 1-59933-049-0; 978-1-59933-049-5

MorningStar's website: www.morningstarministries.org
For information call 1-800-542-0278.

Cover design by Kevin Lepp
Book Layout by Dana Zondory

The silhouette image allegedly of William Tennent is used by permission from
the Presbyterian Historical Society, Philadelphia, PA.

Unless otherwise indicated, all Scripture quotations are taken from the New
American Standard Bible, copyright © 1960, 1962, 1963, 1968, 1971, 1973,
1974, 1977 by The Lockman Foundation. Italics in Scripture are for emphasis
only.

Printed in the United States of America.

TABLE OF CONTENTS

DEDICATION

To my Lord Jesus—for inviting me to walk with You on this thrilling adventure of discovery. And now that this book is published, may I come along on Your next trip? My bags are already packed!

To my wonderful wife, Lisa—for your tender love, patience, and strength. You truly are my **"lily among the thorns" (see Song of Solomon 2:2).**

To my darling daughter, Moriah Elizabeth—for the sweet sunshine you have brought into my life.

To my parents, Robert Hansen and Margaret Murphy—for always thinking the best of me, and showing me **"the way"** in which I should go (see Proverbs 22:6).

<ᕖᕣᕗ>

To Wendy Wirsch, historian for William Tennent's Neshaminy-Warwick Presbyterian Church—for your research and zeal to see Tennent's vision carried on.

<ᕖᕣᕗ>

To Scott Asproth and my "feedback" circle of family and friends—thank you all for your labor of love. You've helped make this book possible!

FOREWORD

The story of William Tennent and his Log College is one of the remarkable stories of both church and American history. The fruit of such a humble enterprise not only helped to set the course of a great nation, but its fruit continues to touch lives generations later. However, few understand the price he paid to see all these things come to pass.

Time and again, church people and fellow ministers misconstrued Tennent's intentions to see people equipped for their ministry call. Financially, he was "poor as a church mouse," proving to the world that money can be one of our least valuable assets. Sickness and death regularly visited his family, but true faith is greater than these. Nevertheless, every test he faced only served to strengthen his resolve to see his Log College vision fulfilled—to equip the church to save America! Few could have imagined that his vision would help save America for generations, and even centuries to come!

By examining both his life and the lives of his Log College revivalists—their successes and failures—we see that Tennent bequeathed a testimony through which we can learn:

• How to be equipped for the call of God on our lives.

• How to minister more effectively within the marketplace, the church, the classroom, and our homes.

• How to raise up Log College-type revivalists, schools, and churches which can equip the church to save the world!

There is a popular saying that "those who do not know history are doomed to repeat it." It certainly has merit, but in this case I think we should consider that we need to understand this history so that we *can* repeat it. The Lord said that faith is like one of the smallest seeds, the mustard seed. This story is one of the great testimonies of how even the smallest seed of vision can grow up to bear unimaginable fruit when coupled with courage and endurance.

—John Hansen and Rick Joyner

"Multiply the Log Colleges—yes multiply the Log Colleges."
—James Beaver, Governor of Pennsylvania (1837-1914)[1]

CHAPTER ONE

THE SIGNIFICANCE

For who has despised the day of small things?
(see Zechariah 4:10 NKJV)

Few people know about William Tennent, even though after three centuries his influence continues to reach worldwide. For those who are familiar with his life, he is recognized for grandfathering over sixty colleges and universities, including Princeton University, through his makeshift Log College. Others know him for fathering the greatest series of spiritual revivals in early America. But few understand the price he paid to see all these things come to pass. Although the circumstances surrounding Tennent's life differ from ours, the lessons taught through his story are both timeless and universal.

THE LEGACY

The Latin engraving on Tennent's tombstone, which is translated *"He built better than he knew,"* leads us to ask: What did he really build? It is true scores of schools and churches trace their roots back to him, but these institutions, as significant as they are, were only by-products of his primary goal. Instead of building institutions, Tennent, through his small Log College, aspired to build anointed Christian leaders who would impact their generation. It was his aim to fashion "living epistles" whose hearts were **"written . . . with the Spirit of the living God" (see II Corinthians 3:3)**. Thus, his mission can be summed up in the words of W.B. Yeats: *"Education is not the filling of a pail, but the lighting of a fire."²*

Tennent's Log College was not a typical school. From its very inception, controversy surrounded everyone associated with it. In the heart of the debate over it lies the answer to this age-old question: What qualifies someone to be a Christian minister? In other words, what is needed to effectively equip and release Christian believers into their God-given callings? To this day, many believe that only those trained in "authorized" schools are qualified to minister. But some, like William Tennent, dared to think otherwise, just as his Savior did when He chose those who seemed to be the least likely to help lead the early church.

Whether we realize it or not, every Christian has received a calling from the Lord. The term "calling" is not synonymous with "career," as is often assumed. Rather, a calling is a supernatural drawing or invitation from God for us to participate with Him in a specific work.³ In fact, our primary calling is to **"be with Him" (see Mark 3:14)**, and out of that relationship with Him will come our call to work with Him. Years may even pass before He reveals to us in what manner He wants us to work. But no matter what, it is our relationship with Him that, as Jesus said, is the **"one thing"** needful above all (see Luke 10:39-42).

Tennent understood that God could equip people in any place, at any time, and with any thing. In other words, only He can make us adequate for the calling wherewith He has called us. **"Not that we are adequate in ourselves,"** wrote the Apostle Paul, **"to consider anything as coming from ourselves, but** *our adequacy is from God, who also made us adequate* **as servants of a new covenant..." (II Corinthians 3:5-6).** It was on this premise that Tennent built his "school of the prophets"—the Log College.

Tennent strongly believed there was more to being a minister of Christ than carrying academic credentials. Although educational pursuits are needful, he understood that they should be secondary to our learning to minister in the **"demonstration of the Spirit and of power" (see I Corinthians 2:4).** Hence, Tennent sought through his school to restore the passion and the power of the gospel in the lives of everyday believers—even at the cost of his reputation.

TO BE TAUGHT OF GOD

From the dawn of creation until now, it has been the Lord's heart that we **"all be taught of God" (see John 6:45).** There is a difference between being taught *about* God and being **"taught of God."** As the founding charter of Harvard University states, the goal of all education is not to acquire more theological knowledge, but to draw closer to the Lord relationally:

Let every student be plainly instructed, and earnestly pressed to consider well the main end of his life and studies is to know God and Jesus Christ which is eternal life (John 17:3), and therefore lay Christ in the bottom, as the only foundation of all sound knowledge and learning.[4]

If you are unsure about what God has called you to be or how to prepare for it, then I pray that He will use this book to **"instruct you and teach you in the way which you should go" (see Psalms 32:8).** If, however, you are already walking in your calling (whether it is in a church organization, business, school, or your family), yet you hunger to see God manifest His power and freedom in the lives of ordinary people, then let this testimony about Tennent speak to you.

American President Benjamin Harrison made a prophetic observation about Tennent's fledgling ministry school worth considering:

I stand dumb before the thought of what the great day will reveal as the fruit of this modest but pious and courageous effort here in the institution of the Log College—the wholesome fruit of faith.[5]

Is this not also what you want from your life—that **"your fruit would remain"?** (**see John 15:16**) *"Books, when read, promote action and form opinions for ages to come,"* wrote one author.[6] It is, therefore, my hope that the following story would not be mere information for you, but a life-changing source of inspiration. And, like William Tennent, may the Lord through you build better than you know.

CHAPTER TWO

HEEDING THE CALL

**I will instruct you and teach you in the way
which you should go (see Psalm 32:8).**

The year 1739 was bittersweet for William Tennent. His troubles began in Philadelphia during his denomination's leadership council meeting, called the Synod. On behalf of the Tennent party, William's eldest son Gilbert objected to the Synod's resolutions enacted the year before. The first of the 1738 resolutions to be challenged involved the Synod's control over where their fellow ministers could preach. The second objection was over the Synod's newly granted power to decide who could be ordained to the ministry. The Tennents foresaw the long-term consequences of the resolutions. To them, they were the death sentence for their family's Log College ministry school—and they had to be repealed.

After much deliberation over the Tennent party's objections, the time came for casting votes. If the Synod voted to continue implementing the controversial resolutions, the implications could potentially prove far-reaching. Much more seemed at stake with this vote than just the survival of an insignificant ministry project. No one there could have dreamed that William Tennent's rustic school would one day father colleges, or that it would directly impact many of America's Founding Fathers, or that a few months later it would stand at the forefront of one of the greatest moves of God in recorded history! With the Synod's vote, the very destiny of the nation seemed to hang in the balance!

POWER STRUGGLES

With a show of hands, a great majority of the Synod members overruled Gilbert's objections and added even heavier stipulations to the prior year's resolutions. An incensed Gilbert voiced that this would *"prevent his father's school for training gracious men for the ministry."*[7] How could he idly stand by while his father's school stood before this ecclesiastical firing squad? His family raised this ministry from its birth. It was the dream into which his father had poured his life for the past twelve years. And what added insult to injury was that this threat came from those who once extended the Tennent family the right hand of fellowship!

Gilbert believed their ruling was nothing short of a conspiracy to shut down the school. But why would anyone want to do that? Did they think heresy was being taught at the Log College? Or that his father was unfit to hold the office of minister? No, it was not that morally clear-cut. This battle was all about control.

Yet, who would have thought that although these ministers were now wrangling over church politics, in a matter of months God would bring the greatest spiritual revival to touch their shores? Perhaps Satan foresaw the coming move of God, and thus sent a preemptive strike to divide them. What a spectacle that Synod meeting must have been to outsiders. To think that here in the "City of Brotherly Love" (Philadelphia), the church's own leaders were feuding.

Jesus said, **"By this all men will know that you are My disciples, if you have love for one another" (John 13:35).** Yet how often have we likewise damaged the church's reputation before the world, because we allowed lesser issues to distract us from God's priorities for us: to love Him and to love one another? (see Matthew 22:37-39)

The Scriptures tell us that whenever strife and disorder surface in relationships it is because someone has **"jealousy and selfish ambition"** in their heart (see I Corinthians 3:3-4; James 3:16). **"The Lord's bond-servant,"** command the Scriptures, **"must not be quarrelsome, but... *with gentleness* correcting those who are in opposition, if perhaps God may grant them repentance leading to the knowledge of the truth, and they may come to their senses and escape from the snare of the devil..." (II Timothy 2:24-26).** We are never to compromise the truth, but we should also be careful *when* and *how* to present the truth. For if we fail to speak **"the truth *in love*,"** we will desecrate the very faith we claim to espouse (see Ephesians 4:15).

Numerous questions must have swirled in Tennent's mind about what he should do next. Should he give his opponents the benefit of the doubt? Was God judging his ministry because he built it on wrong motives? Maybe the Synod ministers wanted the same end as he did—to see believers spiritually equipped—but only by different means. If true, maybe William and Gilbert were overreacting, allowing their suspicious minds to conjure up a make-believe conspiracy.

On the other hand, what if William's suspicions were true—that his fellow ministers were setting him up to fail? If so, and his colleagues had their way, it could mean everything he had invested—his time, his money, and his heart—would lie on the altar of sacrifice. And if this were the case, did God want him to stand his ground and **"fight the good fight of faith"** for the Log College? (see I Timothy 6:12) Should he take up the apostolic defense and confront the Synod with the soul-searching question: "Is it right that I obey you rather than God?" Or should he resign in order to keep peace?

This was only one of the three crucial battles William faced in 1739. Maybe it was no coincidence that the assaults against Tennent greatly intensified soon after he started his Log College. But why was he struggling so much when all he wanted to do was follow God and serve His people? Even though he knew **"our struggle is not against flesh and blood" (see Ephesians 6:12),** the misunderstandings and mistreatments imposed on him must have weighed heavily upon his soul. He wanted to obey **"the heavenly vision"** God placed in his heart, but how much more suffering would he have to endure? (see Acts 26:19)

THE EARLY YEARS

Although the year 1739 was the hardest Tennent had ever faced up to that point, the trials and tests of his earlier life seemed to have prepared him for that critical year. In 1673, William was born in Scotland—a land stained with a bloody history of religious wars. Most in those days believed the freedom of Christian worship to be the highest of all human rights. But deciding which expression of Christianity was the "correct" one was always a point of contention. There were wars between Protestants and Catholics; between Anglican Protestants and Puritan Protestants; and virtually everyone warred against the Dissenters (people such as Presbyterians, Baptists, and Quakers who disagreed with the state church). Sadly, the battle over the gospel essentials still wages between many Christians and churches to this day.

Although history is silent regarding William's childhood, what is known is that at some point William and his younger brother decided to follow their grandfather's footsteps by graduating from the University of Edinburgh and becoming Anglican ministers.

When Tennent first felt God calling him to study for the ministry, heaven knows what he envisioned his future would hold. Would he become like the Scottish hero William "Braveheart" Wallace, who led his people to greater freedom? Or, would he be more like the fiery reformer John Knox, whose very prayers the Queen of Scotland feared *"more than an army of ten thousand men"*?[8] On the other hand, would he become a simple pastor who led **"a tranquil and quiet life in all godliness and dignity,"** as St. Paul described? (see I Timothy 2:2)

His first ministry assignment out of university was as domestic chaplain for the Duchess of Hamilton. By worldly standards, this position seemed promising: His needs were well met, and he associated with royalty. But for reasons unknown, William (in 1701) left not only his comfortable pastorate, but the very land of his birth—all for the greener pastures of Ireland. Soon after arriving in his newfound home, however, he changed denominations and joined the Presbyterians under the Synod of Ulster, the assembly of ministers and elders.

Within the next year, Tennent met a relative of the Duchess named Catherine Kennedy. Catherine's father, Gilbert Kennedy, was a Scottish Presbyterian minister who had escaped to Ireland because of his "nonconformity" to the Established Church. The following spring, William married nineteen year-old Catherine, and in 1703 she bore their firstborn son, Gilbert. Interestingly, the year 1703 was when three future Great Awakening revivalists all came into the world: Gilbert Tennent, a leading Presbyterian revivalist; Jonathan Edwards (1703-58), an internationally known Congregationalist revivalist; and John Wesley (1703-91), the leading founder of the Methodist movement.

Outwardly, William Tennent's life seemed fulfilled. At age thirty, this family man was now living out his heart's desire serving as a minister. But something still left his conscience feeling ill at ease. Ever since his influential Anglican relatives, the Greenshields, had cast seeds of doubt on him about Presbyterianism, William grew uncertain about his choice of faith. Then within a year, those seeds of doubt came to harvest.

In 1704, Tennent succumbed to his relatives' arguments and made a career change. Handing in his resignation to the Presbyterian Church, he set out to become a deacon in the Irish Episcopal Church. Quite possibly, the Greenshields pressured him into this decision because of the Irish Parliament's recent ban on all Dissenting denominations, including Presbyterianism. (Presbyterianism is an expression of Christianity patterned after the works of John Calvin and John Knox.) William's Episcopal relatives, therefore, must have felt having a Presbyterian minister as their kin stained their family crest.

Concurrently, a pamphlet war broke out in Ireland over the legitimacy of Presbyterian marriages, calling them *"licenses for sin"* and Presbyterian children *"bastards."* Presbyterians were even dragged before ecclesiastical courts and excommunicated as *"fornicators."*[9] For the Tennents, this meant in the eyes of the law that their own children were considered illegitimate! Perhaps for his family's reputation, William the nonconformist chose to conform to the Established Church.

A MATTER OF CONVICTION

Was William Tennent wrong to conform to the state church's wishes? Not if he stayed true to the Scriptures and his personal core values (see Romans 14:22; James 4:17). The Apostle Paul, for instance, lived to be **"all things to all men, so that I may by all means save some,"** yet he also refused to conform to anyone's agenda that violated the gospel (see I Corinthians 9:19-22; I Corinthians 10:33; Galatians 2:4-5).

To be an effective witness for the Lord, it is vital that we firmly hold to the clear teachings of Scripture (the Personhood and mission of Jesus, the authority of Scripture, etc.), yet be flexible with beliefs and customs that do not conflict with Scripture. In Tennent's case, he was free in Christ to change churches if he wished, but he was obliged to stay true to the Bible, his convictions, and God's call on his life.

Within two years after his conforming, Tennent climbed the ecclesiastical ladder, moving up from Episcopal deacon to priest. Soon after taking holy orders, he again found himself serving as a domestic chaplain for the nobility. Outwardly, Tennent seemed to come full circle, but inwardly something changed. Although he outwardly conformed, he remained true to his nonconformist convictions. For instance, his sermon *"Because Of Your Unbelief,"* which he preached at his Episcopal ordination and numerous times thereafter, contained the same theme he later taught to his Log College students—that to intellectually believe like a Christian did not make one a Christian. Everyone needs to be **"born again,"** as the Savior Himself said, if we intend to see or enter His kingdom (see John 3:3, 5). Tennent preached:

> [M]*en make again oral profession of the name of Christ as the Turks* [Moslems] *do of Mohammed, because it is the religion professed there when they are born. A man may take up the opinion of a Christian country, and not be one bit better than Turks, Jews, or infidels . . . there may be assent* [to Christian doctrines] *and yet unbelief still. The devils* [also] *assent, as well as know . . . Assent is necessary, but not sufficient.*[10]

In other words, there is a vast difference between intellectually believing like a Christian and knowing Christ Himself experientially. Intellectual Christianity cannot free any of us from our spiritual darkness or bondages. We all need the Savior to *personally* set us free. That is the heart of the gospel.

LIFELESS CHRISTIANITY

Then in 1717, William preached a message that marked the commencement of his lifelong habit of challenging the spirituality of his ministry colleagues:

> *A minister or clergyman may come to the Lord's Supper, and yet not eat the Lord's Supper. He may celebrate it as a minister, and yet not eat it as a sincere Christian. He may eat it because his office obliges him to administer it, and yet not eat it with that sense which becomes a sincere believer.*
>
> *Custom may carry them a great way. . . For they may do it upon the account of their office, and because it is expected of them, but the sense of the end of the love of God may be wanting* [lacking]—*which defect makes it a very lame offering.*[11]

Tennent, in essence, was saying there is a vast difference between practicing Christianity and fellowshipping with Jesus Himself. In fact, Christ prophesied that there was a day coming when many *Christian* practitioners would experience a rude awakening:

"Many will say to Me on that day, 'Lord, Lord, did we not prophesy *in Your name*, and *in*

Your name cast out demons, and *in Your name* perform many miracles?'

"And then I will declare to them, 'I never knew you; depart from Me, you who practice lawlessness'" (Matthew 7:22-23).

Judging by the content of Tennent's above-mentioned sermons (which seemed to be his favorites since he preached them each several times), it seems he tried to deliver the same awakening message that the prophet Ezekiel declared to the clergy of his day:

"[The] priests have done violence to My law and have profaned My holy things; they have made no distinction between the holy and the profane, and they have not taught the difference between the unclean and the clean; and they hide their eyes from My sabbaths, and I am profaned among them" (Ezekiel 22:26).

While Tennent tried to change his colleagues and parishioners, a change gradually occurred in his own heart. And before long, he found himself making two decisions which forever changed the course of his life.

CHAPTER THREE

CUTTING TIES

**The mind of man plans his way,
but the Lord directs his steps (Proverbs 16:9).**

By 1718, William Tennent could boast of carrying a quarter century's ministry experience under his belt, yet something left him feeling discontented. Doubts over some practices and beliefs in the Episcopal denomination steadily *"affected my conscience,"* he later said. Basically, his concerns were over their governmental structure; their *"ceremonial way of worship;"* and their *"practice of Arminian doctrines."*[12] (Arminianism sought to modify the "Reformed" teachings of John Calvin and Presbyterianism. Many denominations today such as Methodists, Free-Will Baptists, Catholics, and Pentecostals reflect Arminian beliefs.)

Besides Tennent's disturbed conscience, the Irish landlords inflated almost everyone's rent, making the cost of living unbearable. William needed to make some decisions soon. Should he suppress his discontentment while hoping for the best, or should he change his circumstances while he could? True to his heart, he made a daring twofold career move.

William's first decision involved his denominational ties. He ministered in the Irish Episcopal Church for fourteen years, but over time he started to question if he had made the right decision. If Tennent resigned from the state church altogether, would he have wasted fourteen precious years of his life by serving a ministry he thought unsuitable for him? Not at all—that is, as long as he did his ". . . **work heartily, as for the Lord rather than for men" (Colossians 3:23).** Just as Jesus implied when Mary "wasted" her perfume by pouring it on His feet, nothing is ever a waste if it is done out of a heart of worship for the Son of God (see John 12:3-8).

Now at age forty-five, it required great faith and humility for William to make a career change—great faith because he would be leaving the security of the state-supported church to rejoin the illegal and financially volatile Presbyterian churches. Great humility was also required of Tennent, because he would have to explain to his Episcopal superiors and church members his reasons for switching ministry loyalties. If he divulged that he differed with their beliefs, would they assume he was implying that not just he, but *they* were in the wrong church? Presumably most of them would disagree with his conclusions.

It should be noted, however, that as far as is known, no one in the Episcopal Church forced Tennent to leave. Perhaps the state church was even content to have him stay, despite (or even because of!) his provocative sermons. Nevertheless, Tennent felt he had to follow his convictions;

and it was time he cut these ties. Besides, by resigning, he was not leaving the ministry altogether, but only one part of the institutionalized church. However, his decision to return to the Presbyterian faith was far less challenging than the next one he made.

WORTH THE RISK?

On top of William's spiritual trials, the Irish economy was spiraling downward, causing many to migrate to America to escape the hardships. For the Tennents, the opportunities of the New World must have sounded promising. If they likewise migrated, at least they had a very influential relative living there. William's cousin James Logan, a Quaker, had become very prosperous through his friendship with Pennsylvania's proprietor, Sir William Penn. Logan served as governor of Penn's colony and mayor of the city of Philadelphia. Surely, having such a prestigious relative as Logan would prove useful to the Tennents.

Of particular interest to William was that a new Presbyterian Synod had recently formed in Philadelphia. A New World, a new Synod, a new ministry, a new life—it all sounded exciting, yet unsettling. The risks of taking his wife and now five children on a two-month voyage across the turbulent Atlantic all for the dream of a better life would probably disturb most. According to one contemporary, children under the age of seven rarely survived transatlantic travel due to the exposure to sickness and the elements. Was it worth the gamble? On the other hand, with Ireland's religious persecution against Dissenters and its exorbitant cost of living, was it more of a gamble for the Tennents to stay right where they were?

William grew accustomed to taking risks in order to head in the direction God seemed to lead him. Perhaps reading such passages as Proverbs 3:5-6 brought much inspiration to this faith-walking family:

Trust in the LORD with all your heart, and do not lean on your own understanding.

In all your ways acknowledge Him, and He will make your paths straight.

While the elder Tennent struggled over his decision to leave the Episcopal Church and Ireland, his fifteen-year-old son, Gilbert, was likewise struggling—but over a far more serious matter. For the last year, young Gilbert had undergone a "dark night of the soul," where he wrestled with his Maker about surrendering his life to Him. Surely, this was a time of great change for all of the Tennents.

Needless to say, William daringly decided to start a new life for his family. Leaving far behind them the securities of the Old World, they sailed westward to the New. And almost as a gift from heaven for their stepping out in faith, Gilbert surrendered his life to Christ while aboard ship. Truly for the Tennents—and especially for young Gilbert— all things became new that year (see II Corinthians 5:17; Revelations 21:5).

FACING THE SYNOD

After weeks aboard ship, their journey ended only to begin anew in Pennsylvania's "City of Brotherly Love"— Philadelphia. It was as if when Pennsylvania's proprietor,

Sir William Penn, referred to the young colony as a *"holy experiment,"* he prophetically described not so much the colony itself, but the journey that Christian immigrants like the Tennents would undergo just to get there.

Soon after landing on September 6, 1718, William chronicled how they were *"courteously entertained by* [his cousin] *Mr. James Logan, agent and secretary of all Pennsylvania."*[13] But Tennent did not come all this way just to be entertained by extended family. About a fortnight later, he appeared before the Presbyterian Synod of Philadelphia, where he sought to publicly renounce his Episcopal ties and request reinstatement to the faith he once embraced.

A committee interviewed him to determine if his reinstatement passed their criteria for clergy membership. Although they were *"well satisfied with his credentials,"* the interview was only half the battle.[14] Now he had to face all the Synod's ministers for final approval.

Tennent's possible reinstatement was the fourth item on the afternoon meeting's agenda. For the twenty-four ministers and elders present, this meeting was probably routine business. But for William it was crucial—his plans hinged on its outcome. If these American Presbyterians rejected his request, what else could he do to make a decent living? He was age forty-five, with a wife and five children to support. His family had come a long way, both geographically and spiritually, just to get to America. Would the Synod's vote now bring this difficult chapter in his life to a close, or only prolong it?

Although Tennent satisfied the committee's inquiry, the Synod had some reservations about admitting him into their membership. Doling out to him a *"serious exhortation to continue steadfast in his now holy profession,"* they also submitted his testimony into public record for future reference—an uncommon practice for new members.[15] Considering his prior defection from the Presbyterian Church, the Synod might have questioned his level of commitment. Yet despite their reservations, the Synod extended him the right hand of fellowship. At their next meeting, Tennent impressed them with a Latin oration, speaking it as if it were his mother tongue.

FINDING HIS PLACE

Little did William realize the challenge which lay ahead when two months later he accepted a pastorate in East Chester, New York. His problems began when the "Society for the Propagation of the Gospel," an Anglican Church organization engaged in *"the conversion of the Negroes, Indians and Dissenters,"* learned of William's forthcoming arrival.[16] Learning that a Dissenting minister was coming to settle in the village, the Society positioned itself to oppose William before he even began his work.

According to the Anglican "Society," the townspeople divided over having a Dissenting minister like Tennent in their midst. To make matters worse, soon after Tennent arrived, John Bartow (the Society's missionary) secured control of East Chester's public meetinghouse. With no church building, limited financial support, and religious contentions brewing among the villagers, what was William to do?

The following year, William called on his influential cousin Logan to persuade the governor of New York to restrain Missionary Bartow's actions. But the royal governor refused to acquiesce. Tennent probably grew disheartened during those two years in his first American assignment, until one day another village (Bedford) offered him a pastorate. Perhaps seeing no other alternative, he accepted their offer, with no indication that things in Bedford would be better than where he was.

When the Tennents relocated to Bedford in 1720, the villagers warmly welcomed them and let William minister unhindered. Compared to his East Chester and Ireland tenures, Bedford must have been refreshing. Also during this time William commenced writing *Hice Libellus* ["Little Book"], where he documented *"matters worthy of being remembered"* for the sake of posterity.[17] But for reasons unknown, William left out two interesting events from those years.

The first incident occurred in 1723, when, much to William's chagrin, his son Gilbert abandoned his ministry studies to pursue the medical field. But this vocational detour was brief, for soon after making his decision, Gilbert rededicated his life to Christ, and resumed his ministry training under his father's tutelage. Two years later, Gilbert graduated from Yale College with a Master of Arts without first obtaining a bachelor's degree! His Yale professors, in fact, prophetically described the young Tennent as *"energetic as a revival preacher."*[18]

For William, seeing his firstborn son—and his first student—excel scholastically and passionately for Christ must have thrilled him beyond words. Those with a true shepherd's heart—whether they are parents, teachers, ministers, or business people—want their underlings to not only succeed, but to exceed their own successes. True mentors understand that it is only when their protégés succeed that they also succeed.

In the same year that Gilbert graduated from Yale, William learned he was being considered for the post of rector at Yale. Although he was eventually denied, he probably felt honored to be considered for the position at the rising Ivy League school.

POOR AS A CHURCH MOUSE

In the midst of these joys, however, William also faced disappointments. While he proved a good steward of heaven's **"true riches,"** his stewardship of earthly riches was another matter (see Luke 16:11). Possibly due to mismanagement or insufficient support from his parishioners, the Tennents overextended themselves financially. Cousin Logan had his opinions about William's financial aptitude, believing *"the man* [to be] *absolutely unskilled in such affairs as craved my direction . . . Poor Tennent understands nothing of the kind* [business], *and therefore perhaps he is poor."*[19]

But was Logan's assessment of Tennent accurate, that he was destitute because he was a poor money manager? In those days, a clergyman's primary source of income was typically from church offerings. This is why many Dissenting ministers oversaw several churches at a time: to support their families, as well as to further the work of God's kingdom. For instance, later in our story Tennent moved to Pennsylvania, where he pastored in the villages of Bensalem, Neshaminy, Deep Run, and Newtown. (Some of these congregations he pastored simultaneously, but not all four at once.)

A letter which Gilbert and others wrote later to a congregation in New Jersey sheds more light on the plight ministers in those days faced:

> *We must remark to you with grief that the poverty and distress of our ministers; and the unkind treatment they meet with from their people discourages parents of affluent circumstances from devoting their children to the service of God in the Gospel ministry. It discourages many of our useful and promising young men from entering into a state attended with so many difficulties...*[The poverty has] *obliged many faithful ministers to remove to the great loss of their worldly interest (small as they are) which they must do rather than starve.*[20]

As for William Tennent, the people of Bedford responded to the needs of their overburdened pastor by giving him over two hundred acres of land. The land was a prized gift, especially considering that he gave *"his attention chiefly to farming,"* while he conducted ministry work during his off hours.[21] It is biblical that some ministers are **"set apart"** exclusively for the work of the gospel (see Acts 13:2; Romans 1:1; I Corinthians 9:1-18), while some, like the Apostle Paul, chose to also work a trade to support their ministry endeavors. As one writer put it,

> *The Greek word used for "set apart" in Romans 1:1 and Acts 13:2 is not the word used for holiness. There is a difference in function between gospel work and ordinary work, but no difference in acceptability before God.*[22]

In other words, if God calls someone to work within a church environment, and He calls another to the marketplace, neither calling is more acceptable in His eyes (see I Corinthians 7:17-24).

In addition to William's support from the village of Bedford, another village in the nearby Connecticut colony supported him with the *"minister's rate"* of salary for several years.[23] Even the Synod of Philadelphia loaned him three-fourths the amount of his annual salary to get him more financially secure. Heaven knows the financial hardships those early ministers suffered to further the cause of Christ. Those college-trained men easily could have entered more lucrative careers than church ministry. Instead, they deemed it far better to store up "**...an unfailing treasure in heaven, where no thief comes near, nor moth destroys**" (Luke 12:33).

NESHAMINY

Nevertheless, despite everyone's generosity, the Tennents were still poor. Something had to be done, for dire straits were again forcing them to seek other horizons. Selling their Bedford real estate holdings, the Tennents moved (in the mid-1720s) to Bucks County, Pennsylvania to fill a Presbyterian pastorate in Bensalem. Although we should avoid making spiritual decisions based solely on our finances, William's move seemed to be the hand of God. Bucks County would become known as the launching pad for the greatest endeavor of his life.

The Tennent's first home in Bucks County (which they rented) suited a minister, for it sat on a main access road between Philadelphia and New York. Since it was customary to provide hospitality to weary travelers, the Tennents had plenty of ministry opportunities. And to their credit, they never stopped giving to others, despite their longstanding poverty.

Then in 1726 in a village called Neshaminy, William gathered a group of settlers together to meet regularly in someone's house during winter and a barn during summer. The following year the congregation decided to build a sanctuary on some land through which a branch of the Neshaminy Creek flowed. The name "Neshaminy," incidentally, is Native American for *"the place where you drink twice,"* referring to its forks.[24]

Thanks to Cousin Logan's fifty-acre land grant and cash gift, the Tennents (in 1729) moved from their rental home to a house of their own. Its location in Northampton was ideal, lying conveniently between the Bensalem and Neshaminy congregations. In the following year, the Synod honored Tennent by appointing him moderator of its annual session. It seemed as if things were falling into place for him.

But within a few short years, Tennent and his sons found themselves facing deadly storms that could have completely shipwrecked their futures. Yet, as only God can do, those storms instead transformed his young student-sons into revivalists.

CHAPTER FOUR

THE FIRST REVIVALISTS

...if one generation begins to decline, the next that follows usually grows worse, and so on, till God pours out his Spirit again upon them.

—*Samuel Willard (1640-1707), vice president of Harvard*[25]

S hortly before death began to strike against the Tennent household, God introduced William's son, Gilbert, to a man whom many (like Revivalist George Whitefield) called *"the beginner of the great work"* known as the Great Awakening.[26] His name was Theodorus Frelinghuysen (1692-1747), a fiery Dutch-Reformed minister whose zeal both offended and convicted all who heard him. And among those deeply convicted was the young Gilbert.

When Frelinghuysen arrived in New Jersey from the Netherlands in 1720, he found the Christianity of the Dutch settlers reduced to *"formalism and self-righteousness,"* wrote an associate of his.[27]

The necessity of a new heart had almost entirely been lost sight of ... Christians were not ashamed to ridicule Christian experience, and many had become very resolute in opposing it ... The church was attended at convenience, and religion consisted of the mere formal pursuit of the routine of the day.

William Tennent, Jr. agreed with this assessment of the Raritan Valley, saying that:

[The New Birth] *was made a common game of; so that not only the preachers but professors of that truth were called in derision "new born" and looked upon as holders forth of some new and false doctrine.*[28]

Frelinghuysen wasted no time confronting the prevalent complacency by probing people with the question: *"Have you then, with the utmost care examined, whether you be born again?"*

With an evangelistic flair, he would appeal to his listeners *"to be willing, and to arise and come to Jesus."* Moreover, before he officiated the sacrament of communion, he announced that only the *"penitent, believing, upright, and converted persons"* were eligible to participate.[29] To have it otherwise would disgrace the Savior's sacrificial death. As expected, Frelinghuysen's stirring message produced two responses from people—they either resented him or repented.

CONFRONTING COMPLACENCY

Frelinghuysen believed that *"neither a thorough literary course, nor an ecclesiastical licensure, nor a lawful call constitute us* [as] *faithful watchmen.*"[30] This did not set well with his ministerial colleagues, especially when he publicly judged some of them as *"unconverted ministers.*"[31] Not surprisingly, some clerics and church members denounced him for allegedly preaching heresy, and drafted a 146-page complaint signed by sixty-four families to submit to his superiors. One time some of Frelinghuysen's disgruntled church members locked him out of two of his four churches! Surely this persecuted pastor took comfort in these words of Jesus:

> **"They will make you outcasts from the synagogue, but an hour is coming for everyone who kills you to think that he is offering service to God.**
>
> **"And these things they will do, because they have not known the Father or Me" (John 16:2-3).**

By the following year (1726—the year the Tennents moved to Neshaminy), undeniable fruit appeared in Frelinghuysen's ministry. Conversions occurred among the young and the poor, as well as among his church elders and deacons. Before long, his four churches overflowed with people. By 1727, a full-blown revival swept New Jersey's Raritan Valley. Even churches outside of his denomination invited him to preach.

In like manner, Frelinghuysen generously opened his own pulpit to the young Presbyterian pastor—Gilbert Tennent. The Dutch Reformed revivalist even encouraged his church members to support Gilbert's work. At times, the two ministers spoke in succession to the same congregation. Although they were from different denominations, their common-union in Christ superceded any theological differences they may have had. At one point, Frelinghuysen and four other Dutch-Reformed ministers defended Gilbert's ministry before their superiors in Amsterdam, stating that *"some of our adherents attend his* [Tennent's] *services and help support him, we neither can, nor ought to, forbid."*[32] Theirs was a true partnership in the gospel work.

Although the Dutch-Reformed denomination required its ministry candidates to be licensed back in Amsterdam, Frelinghuysen instead resolved to train and equip future leaders locally. He began by turning his church "helpers" into lay preachers, and later delegated to some of them his pastoral duties, with the exception of officiating the communion table. He even allowed his leaders to oversee the church services in his absence. Furthermore, he envisioned planting an American ministry school, which his son fulfilled by helping lay the groundwork for Queens College (now Rutgers University).

But heaven intended more for Gilbert and Frelinghuysen than just a trans-denominational working relationship. Although Gilbert learned the New Birth theology from his father, he needed to learn from Frelinghuysen how to promote it among the masses. Moreover, Frelinghuysen and his Dutch-Reformed people had such a passion for Christ and the Scriptures that it provoked Gilbert to godly jealousy (see II Corinthians 11:2; Hebrews 10:24). Gilbert recalled:

> *When I came there . . . I had the pleasure of seeing much of the fruits of his* [Frelinghuysen's] *ministry. Divers of his hearers . . . appeared to be converted persons,*

*by their soundness in principle, Christian experience, and
pious practice....*

*This, together with a kind letter which he sent me
respecting the necessity of dividing the word aright, and
giving to every man his portion in due season, through
the divine blessing, excited me to greater earnestness in
ministerial labors. I began to be very much distressed about
my want [lack] of success. For I knew not, for half a year
or more after I came to New Brunswick, that any one was
converted by my labors, although several persons were at
times affected transiently.*[33]

In comparison to Frelinghuysen, Gilbert saw a lack in
his life. He felt powerless, and the fruits of his labors proved
it. But the mere knowledge of his powerlessness was not
enough. Something deeper needed to be worked into his soul.
Gilbert had to come to the end of himself—and as has been
said, *"Man's extremity is the Lord's opportunity."*[34]

DEATH THREATS

When William Tennent's three eldest sons, Gilbert,
William Jr., and John, started pursuing the call of God on
their lives, they probably assumed they had a whole lifetime
ahead of them to work for God. But as they soon learned,
the ways of man are not always God's ways. In their case, He
allowed them to undergo deep suffering, so that **"those
things which can be shaken"** in their lives would fall away
and **"those things which *cannot* be shaken may remain"
(see Hebrews 12:27).** And Gilbert was the first to be shaken.

Although the Tennent brothers heard numerous times
from their father about mankind's sinful nature and each

man's need to surrender to Christ, it seems these young ministers needed more than theological instruction. They needed an encounter with God—the kind that transforms teaching into reality, from "water to wine," so to speak (see John 2). If these young men wanted **"the power of His resurrection"** to manifest through them, they also needed to know **"the fellowship of His sufferings" (see Philippians 3:10).** Gilbert described what happened:

> *It pleased God to afflict me about the time with sickness, by which I had affecting views of eternity. I was then exceedingly grieved that I had done so little for God, and was very desirous to live for one half year more, if it was His will, that I might stand upon the stage of the world, as it were, and plead more faithfully for His cause, and take more earnest pains for the conversion of souls....*
>
> *I therefore prayed to God that He would be pleased to give me one half year more, and I was determined to endeavor to promote His kingdom with all my might* [through] *all adventures.*[35]

Gilbert's near-death experience convinced him that possessing correct doctrine was insufficient for salvation. What people needed was not so much to be convinced about living more ethically, but about being converted—by experiencing the New Birth.

Soon after, William Jr. and John also faced death's door when they contracted tuberculosis. Gilbert recalled how John's *"conviction of sin, and the state of danger and misery he was brought into by it, was the most violent in degree of any that ever I saw."*[36] Instead of consoling his brother as most would naturally do, Gilbert learned to be careful to not counteract the work of conviction in John's life. John needed to see that although he was not a notorious sinner, he was still a sinner who needed Christ to save him from his sins and hell. Gilbert observed that John's deep remorse

> ...*serves to confute that vain notion of some carnal people that if persons have not been profane in their lives, then they say there is no need of deep convictions, and great anguish of soul, in order to* [come to] *a true closure with Christ.*

Gilbert continued: It was four days later that John *"spoke to me in these words: 'O brother, the Lord has come in mercy to my soul. I was begging Him for a crumb of mercy with the dogs, and Christ has told me that He will give me a crumb.'"* A highly respected gentleman who witnessed the young man's struggles reported how *"the sight of these things was enough to convince an atheist of the reality of religion."*[37] Needless to say, John's testimony became Gilbert's model for preaching deep repentance and the salvation experience.

RAISED FROM THE DEAD

Then there was the extraordinary account of young William Jr.'s death and resurrection after three days. Thanks to the research of the Tennent family's illustrious friend Elias Boudinot, who served as president of the Continental Congress and first president of the American Bible Society, William's death experience is considered credible. William had all the accompanying signs of death—cold skin, stiff body, sunken eyes, stiff mouth, and no breath for three days.

What's more, after he came back to life, he recounted later to Boudinot what he saw during his death experience:

I saw an innumerable host of happy beings, surrounding the inexpressible glory, in acts of adoration and joyous worship; but I did not see any bodily shape or representation in the glorious appearance. I heard things unutterable. I heard their songs and hallelujahs of thanksgiving and praise with unspeakable rapture. I felt joy unutterable and full of glory.

I then applied to my conductor, and requested leave to join the happy throng; on which he tapped me on the shoulder, and said, "You must return to the earth." This seemed like a sword through my heart. In an instant I recollect to have seen my brother [Gilbert] standing before me, disputing with the doctor.

The three days during which I had appeared lifeless, seemed to me to be not more than ten or twenty minutes. The idea of returning to this world of sorrow and trouble gave me such a shock that I fainted repeatedly . . . Such was the effect on my mind of what I had seen and heard, that if it be possible for a human being to live entirely above the world and the things of it, for sometime afterward I was that person. The ravishing sounds of the songs and hallelujahs that I heard, and the very words that were uttered, were not out of my ears, when awake, for at least three years.[38]

These encounters with death became the Tennent brothers' defining moments. For the remainder of young John Tennent's life—which only lasted three more years—he preached what Gilbert called:

...the terrors of an offended Deity, the threats of a broken law, the miseries of a sinful state...[T]*his subject...*[John] *insisted upon because he found it by experience...the most effectual and successful means to alarm the secure sinners.*[39]

For the young Tennents, the apostolic approach for turning people to God was to preach "the terrors," that is, that everyone who publicly or privately sins against God's holiness standards (His Old Testament Law) is subject to His wrath. This concurred with the elder Tennent's conviction, that *"the law is one excellent school master to lead us to Christ"*[40] (see Galatians 3:24). And preaching "the terrors" became the controversial trait of the graduates of Tennent's "school of the prophets."

CHAPTER FIVE

SCHOOL OF
THE PROPHETS

*Education is not the filling of a pail, but the
lighting of a fire.*

—*William Butler Yeats (1865-1939), poet*[41]

Outwardly, his life's purpose seemed nearly complete. So far, William Tennent had successfully schooled his three eldest sons and a young man named Samuel Blair (1712-1751) for the ministry. In addition to pastoring several congregations, William was now mentoring his youngest son Charles. However, once Charles was licensed for the ministry, what else was there for William to look forward to? Did God have any more assignments for the aging preacher?

In the autumn of 1735, the Tennents took a step of faith by upgrading from their fifty-acre home in Northampton to a one-hundred acre plantation in Warminster. Their new homestead rested on busy York Road, a mile from the Neshaminy church. One would expect that at their age they would prefer a simpler and quieter place to live out their days. But this couple refused to grow old in their thinking. This was not their time to retire but to re-fire! And as it turned out, God did have another assignment for them. It was time for them to start the Log College.

CHANGING THE TRAINING

Although William had preached against dead spirituality ever since his Episcopal days, he knew something on a larger scale was needed to turn his country to God. What was needed was, firstly, for people to shake off their apathy; and secondly, for his colleagues to see the New Birth experience as the key to saving the nation. But how could one man bring about this nationwide shaking?

Tennent's answer was simple, but not easy—change the way ministers were trained. Two issues disturbed him the most about the current state of ministry training. First, if someone in the middle and southern colonies felt God's call into professional ministry, most likely he could not afford the schooling. At the time, Presbyterian and Congregational churches in America primarily accepted ministry training through European and New England universities. Considering the high tuition and travel costs, post-secondary education became too expensive for many colonists to pursue, which is probably why William homeschooled his sons for the ministry.

The second and more disturbing issue Tennent faced was the lack of fiery, "born-again" ministers. True, planting local and affordable schools would boost the number of new preachers, but that would not solve the main problem— the church of Christ needed born-again, Spirit-empowered leaders. To Tennent, the universities were producing passionless ministers who preached more to people's heads than to their hearts. In his famed message, *"The Danger of an Unconverted Ministry,"* Tennent's son, Gilbert, poignantly compared the unconverted ministers of his day with the notorious Pharisees of the Bible, remarking how *"they were presently put into the priest's office, though they had no experience of the New Birth."*[42]

The term New Birth, which Gilbert called *"the foundation of practical religion,"* originated with Christ's declaration to an unconverted minister named Nicodemus, that only those who were **"born again"** could see and enter His kingdom (see John 3:3-6).[43] The Apostle Peter likewise affirmed the New Birth as the prerequisite to our experiencing the resurrection power of Christ (see I Peter 1:3).

Most people in eighteenth century America and Europe mistakenly believed they were Christians because they were christened, practiced good deeds, lived morally, or ascribed to certain church creeds. Early Harvard president and Yale's primary founder, Increase Mather, observed that the colonists were *"only civil and outwardly conformed to good order by reason of their education, but never knew what the new birth means."*[44] Needless to say, whenever someone preached the New Birth as the defining point of salvation—apart from religious merit or doctrinal conformity—many were offended.

The revivalists, however, placed the blame for the rampant spiritual ignorance on their clerical colleagues, who emphasized doctrinal conformity over having a personal relationship with Jesus Christ. George Whitefield, a revivalist and friend of the Tennents, summed up the sentiments of his fellow revivalists:

> *For I am persuaded the generality of preachers talk of an unknown and unfelt Christ. The reason why congregations have been so dead is, because they had dead men preaching to them. O that the Lord may quicken and revive them! How can dead men beget living children?*[45]

Imagine how insulted a minister would feel if someone told him that his entire life's work of religious devotion was all in vain if he never experienced Christ's new birth. Even more offensive, if that minister was never born again, he was no better off than a heathen person heading for hell!

On the other hand, if the colonists—and especially the ministers—were converted, their lives would drastically change, and the downward spiritual trend should reverse. This is why the Tennents believed so strongly that the key starting place for saving the nation was to change the ministry training.

BIRTHING A SCHOOL

It is plausible that it was back during the Synod meeting of 1729 that William first got the idea to plant a ministry school. All of the ministers, including Tennent, believed they needed *"to plant a seminary of learning among themselves"* for the purpose of educating *"their young candidates for the ministry."* But they tabled the plan *"partly* [due to] *the infancy, and partly the poverty of their* [ministers'] *circumstances,* [that] *render them unable...."*[46] But that seed-thought about planting a school germinated over time in Tennent's heart, until in 1735 it finally took form.

Since drastic times often call for drastic measures, Tennent felt compelled to think outside the current educational box. Why could he not offer local, affordable ministry schooling right in his own home? Back in the Old Country, academies and private apprenticeships for many professions, including the ministry, were fairly common. Still, it was one thing for William to homeschool his sons, but quite another to start a school.

At this point, William probably applied Matthew 15:33-34 and focused not on what he lacked but on what he had. For one thing, he fluently spoke the classical languages of Latin, Hebrew, and Greek—a needed skill for obtaining ministry licensure. He was also well-versed in biblical doctrines, and had years of ministry experience from which to draw. And, above all—he knew Jesus experientially. Additionally, the proof that Tennent could successfully homeschool people for the ministry was his own sons. Why then could he not expand upon what he was already doing? Moreover, what if God turned his school into another **"school of Tyrannus,"** the biblical training center which impacted the nations? (see Acts 19:9-10) Through one student at a time, William could then help turn the widespread apathy around.

William knew, however, that the task of equipping believers as revivalists was a long-term process. He might have assumed he would never live to see the American church revived, but this was not to be his concern. Tennent simply needed to work at what God assigned to him, and let

God take care of his future. Filled with vision, William laid out his plan for launching his school for revivalists.

SCHOOL OF THE PROPHETS

When the Tennents moved into their new home in 1735, it was the perfect time for them to graduate his "home-school" into a formal training center. Felling trees from the surrounding forest, the Tennents constructed a two hundred square foot log cabin in close proximity to their farmhouse.[47] According to revivalist-friend George Whitefield, this Log College received its name as a mark of derision by Tennent's clerical colleagues. Since the school lacked some key features of eighteenth century colleges—such as a sizeable library and faculty—the Synod's clergy held no high expectation of Tennent's graduates. But Whitefield did not share their shortsightedness, saying the College *"seemed to resemble the schools of the old prophets."*[48]

The phrase "schools of the prophets" refers to the schools found in the biblical towns of Bethel (Hebrew: "house of God"), Naioth ("house of learning"), and Jericho (meaning unknown). Seasoned prophets such as Elisha and Samuel, who trained their protégés in prophecy, homiletics, and music, headed these ancient schools. These schools were informal and built upon relationships, like "schools" of fish.

Prior to his building the Log College, Tennent let his pupils live with his family. Soon after arriving, new students realized that this mentoring program was not all lecture and study. By working and eating alongside his family, the students received an impartation of their teacher's heart. Tennent became their role model, allowing them to see how he preached, how he treated his wife and children, how he treated his neighbors, how he spent his money, and how he spent his time with the Lord. Although William carried the bulk of the training, his wife Catherine acted as his "silent partner" and mother figure for the students. All this personal attention was just what his future revivalists needed.

REVIVALIST CURRICULUM

By examining the schedule of Tennent's alma mater— University of Edinburgh—and of the schools his students started later, it is assumed the Log College's daily curriculum included Hebrew, Greek, Latin, logic, philosophy, theology, homiletics (preaching techniques), and ecclesiology (the nature and functions of the church). Accessing the life accomplishments of his graduates (which are discussed later), Tennent must have highly stressed these subjects. One graduate of the school said a few students graduated in less than five years, but *"most of us have taken a much longer space and time to learn."*[49]

Tennent knew, however, there was more to ministry training than learning theology and ecclesiology. *"Education,"* observed one poet, *"is not the filling of a pail, but the lighting of a fire."*[50] Tennent's students needed what Gilbert described as *"both piety and learning,"* a passion for God and His purposes to complement their academics.[51] In time, the young revivalists matured into men likened to Apollos of old—men who were **"mighty in the Scriptures,"** as well as **"fervent in spirit"** for Jesus Christ **(see Acts 18:24-25)**. In sum, the Log College was a place where the curriculum provided the "meat," and their teacher the "fire."

Because Tennent understood that the purpose of the Word of God was to lead people to the God of the Word, he taught his students to use God's *"one excellent school master"* (Old Testament Law) to show people their failure to follow Him; and their need for His New Birth.[52] In summary, they sought to use God's Law to bring about New Testament conversions. Matthew Henry (1662-1714), a biblical commentator whom early Presbyterians greatly admired, also emphasized the use of Old Testament holiness laws in evangelism:

> *Unfruitful Christians must be awakened by the terrors of the law, which breaks up the fallow ground, and then encouraged by the promises of the gospel, which are warm and fattening, as manure to the tree. Both methods must be tried; the one prepares for the other, and all little enough.*[53]

It must be emphasized, however, that the message of Jesus Christ should never be presented in a condemning manner that excludes God's goodness. As the Apostle Paul told us, **"the *kindness* of God leads you to repentance,"** and we are to **"behold then the kindness *and* severity of God" (see Romans 2:4; 11:22).** Whenever we minister to others, it is fundamental Christianity to preach both His kindness and His severity. To proclaim one exclusive of the other is to preach an unbalanced gospel and a sheer misrepresentation of the Savior. And above all, we should never forget that it is the Holy Spirit's task—and not ours—to convict people of their sins (see John 16:8).

As for the Log College students, preaching "the terrors" became the core of their training, for as their mentor taught:

"God teaches the soul He brings to Christ that liberty from sin is the greatest business in the world." [54]

DOCTRINE TO DYNAMIC

Tennent knew that only God could make **"His ministers a flame of fire"** (see Hebrews 1:7). Yet, because God called him **"for the equipping of the saints for the work of service"** (see Ephesians 4:12), it was his responsibility to train believers in the following four areas:

1. Their character

2. Their vision/calling

3. Their gifting

4. Their theology

Character building was foundational in the Log College curriculum. The stronger a student's foundation was, the more he could handle—and that foundation had to be Christ. **"But each man must be careful how he builds on it** [the foundation]," wrote the Apostle Paul. **"For no man can lay a foundation other than the one which is laid, which is Jesus Christ" (I Corinthians 3:10-11).** Considering what Tennent's graduates achieved later in life, it appears he took great care in how he helped build their lives.

Although each person was responsible for seeking God's plan for his life, their mentor was responsible for polishing their gifts and teaching them new skills. But once they were released into their ministry call, the students should have kept in mind that man's credentials are nothing compared with heaven's credentials. The mark of a true minister of the Lord is not so much where they went to school or to church, but whether they bear His credentials, which are **"...written not with ink but with the Spirit of the living God, not on tablets of stone but on tablets of human hearts" (II Corinthians 3:3).**

Tennent understood, most likely through the Apostles Peter and Paul, that grounding his students in sound biblical theology would potentially safeguard them from sin and heresy (see II Peter 3:15-16; Ephesians 4:11-14). Consequently, their future listeners likewise would be potentially safeguarded (see I Timothy 4:15-16). This is why Presbyterian ministers leaned heavily on the 1648 "Westminster Confession of Faith" and its Catechisms. These were their statements of faith, designed to condense all revealed biblical truth to a series of statements for easy learning. In fact, Presbyterian ministers were expected not only to know and subscribe to the Westminster Confession, but also to teach their parishioners to do the same. However, to what degree people were to subscribe to the creed stirred up many debates.

Although church leaders obviously ought to be tested for scriptural soundness, many fail to see that *anyone* who is called of God ought to know how to **"...contend earnestly for the faith which was once for all handed down to the saints" (Jude 3).** The more we all are grounded in God's Word and allow Him to change us into His image, the less likely we will become like **"the untaught and the unstable [who] distort...Scriptures" (see II Peter 3:16).** This is why Gilbert and other ministers typically forbade *"young converts to take upon them*[selves] *authoritatively to instruct and exhort publicly,"* for it *"tends to introduce the greatest errors, and the greatest anarchy and confusion."*[55] This is not to say young converts should be prevented from ministering to others, but that they should not be placed in a leadership position prematurely for the safety of themselves and others.

It must be said, however, if we do not learn to walk in the Holy Spirit (see Galatians 5:16, 25), then correct theology *by itself* becomes pointless and powerless. When we walk in obedience to the Holy Spirit, He will cause us to **"not carry out the desire of the flesh"**, as well as guide us **"into all the truth" (see Galatians 5:16; John 16:13).** In fact, to **"walk by the Spirit" (see Galatians 5:25)** is the ultimate act of worship that any Christian can offer the Lord.

As for theology, it is nothing more than our knowing who God is and who we are in relation to Him. As Jonathan Edwards poetically analogized about theology:

> [It] *is not he that has learned a long description of the sweetness of honey that can be said to have the greatest understanding of it, but he that has tasted.*[56]

In other words, theological studies should move us from instruction to a deeper devotion to Him, where we regularly encounter the Author of the Book of books. This has been the heart of the Lord since the beginning of time, that we **"all be taught of God" (see John 6:45),** not just about Him, but by Him firsthand.

All this, in short, was William Tennent's answer to the rampant apathy—equip born-again, Spirit-empowered believers to manifest **"...the sweet aroma of the knowledge of Him in every place" (II Corinthians 2:14).** But unfortunately, some were not pleased with how Tennent went about doing this.

THE VISION THAT CHANGED A NATION:
THE LEGACY OF WILLIAM TENNENT

A 19ᵗʰ century artist's rendition of Tennent's Log College. (Murphy, Thomas. *The Presbytery of the Log College; or the Cradle of the Presbyterian Church in America.* Philadelphia: Presbyterian Board of Publication and Sabbath-School Work, 1889, p. i.)

CHAPTER SIX

UNQUALIFIED FOR MINISTRY?

...but our competence comes from God.

He has made us competent as ministers of a new covenant... (II Corinthians 3:5-6 NIV).

William Tennent had faced opposition before, but none so intense as the years following his opening the Log College. In the summer of 1736, a committee from the Philadelphia Presbytery came to his new plantation home to examine his youngest son Charles for licensure. (A presbytery is a council of ministers and elders from a group of churches.) The patriarch's heart must have swelled at the sight of his son following his example into the ministry. Charles' exams also happened to be a personal test for William, because Charles' competency reflected William's training skills.

But, even in the midst of this memorable moment, something else was on William's mind. He had a crucial question to ask the committee, so he waited patiently until the exams ended before bringing up the subject.

TENNENTS ON TRIAL

Young Charles had prepared many years for this day. For Section One of his exams, he gave *"an exegesis in Latin on the question 'An Christus sit solus mundi servitor?'"* (translated, "Is Christ alone the servant or Savior of the world?") For Section Two, Charles delivered a sermon on II Corinthians 5:17, about being a new creation in Christ, where the old passes away and all things become new. This happened to be the heart of William's training—the new birth. For Section Three, the committee checked for Charles' *"ability in prayer"* and *"the languages"* (Latin, Greek, and Hebrew), and his understanding of *"the arts and sciences, especially theology and . . . Scripture."* They also examined him for *"evidences of the graces of sanctification in his soul, of the purity and piety of his intentions."*[57]

At the end of the three-day exams, the committee recorded how William confided to them the issue that shook his confidence:

> *Mr. William Tennent for some reasons proposed to the committee whether he may not be esteemed the proper pastor of the congregation at Neshaminy where he now officiates.*

It may seem ludicrous that William would ever question the validity of the last ten years of his pastoral work. However, a factional group in his Neshaminy church had recently created quite a commotion by seeking his removal. After consideration, the committee ruled about William:

> *...notwithstanding there was never a formal installment of Mr. Tennent among that people ... yet*

on consideration that he was formally called by them and accepted their call, [that] *his maintenance owned him to be their minister, that they did once, the body of them, when this question was proposed to them, openly in the Meeting House, own him as such, that he has for ten years past carried on all the parts of the Gospel ministry among them without opposition . . . and all have submitted to it, he has been all along and still is the proper Gospel minister and pastor of said people.*[58]

These words must have greatly relieved the troubled pastor, but unfortunately the matter remained unsettled. The factional group would not surrender so easily.

TEST OF ENDURANCE

Soon after the next presbytery meeting, *"a supplicant from diverse persons of Mr. William Tennent's congregation"* argued before Tennent's colleagues that he *"was no more than a supply* [a temporary fill-in] *to the said people."* Would the presbytery overrule the favorable decision the committee made back in William's home? Again, to his relief the presbytery upheld the committee's ruling—he was indeed *"the proper legal minister of the said people."*[59]

But the factional group again refused defeat. The next day, they appealed to the Synod, hoping to overturn the presbytery's ruling. It is always disgraceful whenever a servant of the Lord has to defend himself against those he came to serve in matters that do not involve sin or gross misconduct. The Apostle Paul warned us that we should avoid striving and disputing over nonessential legalities, **"for they are unprofitable and worthless" (see Titus 3:9)**. William must have taken great consolation in the Apostle James' encouragement:

Consider it all joy, my brethren, when you encounter various trials,

knowing that the testing of your faith produces endurance.

And *let endurance have its perfect result,* **so that you may be perfect and complete, lacking in nothing (James 1:2-4).**

In the afternoon of May 17, 1736, William stood trial before the Synod, the highest presbyterian ruling body in the land at that time. Again, he had to answer the charges the factional group leveled against him. But this time Tennent stood not alone, for representatives from his presbytery took his defense. Would the Synod uphold the presbytery's verdict and recognize him as Neshaminy's pastor? To William's relief, the Synod unanimously voted:

[to] *justify the judgment of the Presbytery of Philadelphia . . . that said appellants* [the factional group] *had no just cause of complaining against or appealing from said judgment of the presbytery.*[60]

William was vindicated, and the case was closed—but not for long.

Days after his victory at the Synod, William's presbytery licensed his son Charles to *"preach the Gospel where Providence may give him opportunity and call."* [61] For William, Charles' licensing was an additional vindication, showing to all that he could effectively equip people for the ministry.

Moreover, in that same year another of William's Log College students, David Alexander was licensed. Now with six graduates (his four sons, Blair, and Alexander) released into ministry and the Neshaminy issue resolved, William's ministry became more established. But his joy was short-lived.

CHURCH POLITICS

In the spring of 1737, nine months after William's vindication, the factional group submitted to the Synod another petition similar to the one overruled the year before. But this time, some of Tennent's supporting church members came to his defense by countering the faction's charges. After the Synod examined both sides of the issue, it ruled that the factional group's charges:

> ...*in justification of their non-compliance with the Synod's judgment in relation to them last year, and their desire to be freed from Mr. Tennent as their pastor, are utterly insufficient, being founded, (as appears to us) partly upon ignorance and mistake, and partly, (as we fear) upon prejudice.*
>
> *It is therefore ordered that the moderator* [of the Synod] *recommend it to said people* [the factional group] *to lay aside such groundless dissatisfactions, and return to their duty, which they have too long strayed from. Otherwise the Synod will be bound in duty to treat them as disorderly.*[62]

What a relief for William that his colleagues and some of his church people came to his defense! What is more, since the Synod used such words as "prejudice" and "disorderly" to describe the faction's behavior, we can see how this episode manifested the faction's underlying motives— jealousy and selfish ambition, **"for where jealousy and selfish ambition exist, there is disorder and every evil thing" (James 3:16).** This should come as no surprise, since Scripture tells us that **"factions"** are a deed **"of the flesh... [and] those who practice such things will not inherit the kingdom of God" (see Galatians 5:19-21).**

Again, it is one thing to try to remove a leader based on his involvement in a blatant sin, major misconduct, or fundamental doctrinal error; it is quite another to remove a leader just because someone does not like his style. In Tennent's case, why did Neshaminy's disgruntled people not move to another congregation or start their own church? Instead, they refused **"to be subject to rulers, to authorities, to be obedient,"** and therefore defied the biblical exhortation to be **"diligent to preserve the unity of the spirit in the bond of peace" (Titus 3:1; Ephesians 4:3).** It is in cases like this that the Apostle Paul advises to **"reject a** *factious* **man after a first and second warning, knowing that such a man is perverted and is sinning, being self-condemned" (Titus 3:10-11).**

The last week of May 1738 proved pivotal for several reasons. It started with the presbytery offering Tennent to preach periodically to the Newtown congregation, rotating his pulpit time with another minister, Francis McHenry. For Tennent, the Newtown opportunity was at least a reprieve from the church politics at Neshaminy.

The day after the Newtown offer, the Synod approved a controversial overture—which I call the Itinerancy

Act—allowing all ministers to freely preach to any congregation, including those that lay within another presbytery's boundaries, as long as no other pastor had been assigned there. However, if a minister objected to a visiting minister preaching in a vacant pulpit that lay within the objecting minister's presbytery boundaries, the visiting preacher needed to ask permission first from that presbytery or the Synod.

For instance, suppose a church had been without a leader for some time, and someone invited a Presbyterian minister to preach in a church building or barn within the bounds of a certain presbytery. If another minister of that presbytery (who may even live a hundred miles away), disagreed with the visiting minister's visit, then that minister could charge the visiting minister with committing "intrusion."

For the Synod, this Act was a good method for promoting ministerial courtesy. But some—especially the Log College sympathizers—saw this regulation more as territorial preservation than courtesy.

Then, the Log College supporters scored a victory when the Synod permitted the New York Presbytery to create an offshoot called the New Brunswick Presbytery. Because most of Tennent's supporters dominated this new presbytery, they now had, according to Gilbert, the mechanism to credential revivalists. But their victory lasted only a few days.

QUALIFIED FOR MINISTRY?

Three days after the creation of the New Brunswick Presbytery, the Presbytery of Lewes introduced another controversial act, which ultimately triggered the splitting of their denomination. This proposal (which I call the Examining Act) addressed a candidate's qualifications for the ministry. The Tennent men attentively listened as the clerk read the proposal. Most, if not all of the ministers agreed with the Act's premise, that they lacked a coordinated effort to effectively equip people for their callings, and most colonists could not afford to *"spend a course of years in the European or New England colleges."*

But as the clerk continued reading, the Act created a convincing argument against certain educational projects such as the Log College.

> *For we know that natural parts, however great and promising, for want* [lack] *of being well improved, must be marred of their usefulness, and cannot be so extensively serviceable to the public, and that want* [lack] *of due pains and care paves the way for ignorance, and this for a formidable train of sad consequences.*

It is sad whenever someone endowed with great intelligence or gifting intentionally buries them, instead of using them for God's purposes (see Matthew 25:14-30). People could become unprofitable or *"marred of their usefulness"* if they are not provided with good training. But when the proposal came to its point, we can see how the Presbytery of Lewes used this line of reasoning to make such schools as the Log College subservient to the Synod:

> *To prevent this evil* [of ignorance], *it is humbly proposed as a remedy that every student who had not studied with approbation* [with approved schooling], *passing the usual courses in some of the New England or*

European colleges approved by public authority, shall before be encouraged by any presbytery for the sacred work of the ministry, apply himself to this Synod, and that they [the presbytery] *appoint a committee of their members yearly whom they know to be well skilled in the several branches of philosophy and divinity and the languages, to examine such students in this place, and finding them well accomplished in those several parts of learning, shall allow them a public testimonial from the Synod, which, till better provision be made, will in some measure answer the design of taking a degree in the college.*

And for encouragement of students let this be done, without putting them to further expenses than attending. And let it be an objection against none, where they have read [studied]*, or what books, but let all encouragement be only according to merit.*[63]

This Act seemed like a reasonable compromise, attempting to negate any prejudice against privately educated ministry candidates. In addition, it sent a church-wide message that institutionalized ministry training was not the sole requirement for licensure. And William, being university-trained himself, knew the benefits of securing a solid education.

The problem, however, was that the Act insinuated that training opportunities, such as one-on-one mentorships and schools like the Log College, were substandard to university training. Here is the list of academic disciplines in which the Synod required all ministry candidates to possess a sufficient proficiency:

1. physics (an archaic term for anatomy and physiology);

2. ethics (morality and social manners);

3. metaphysics (the relationship between mind and matter);

4. pneumatics (the relationships between spiritual substances, such as God, angels, and men's souls);

5. critics (literary criticism).

According to the Synod, Tennent did not highly stress these five disciplines in his school, because he *"cannot or doth not teach"* them.[64] But to the credit of this one-man faculty, at least Tennent was able to impart to his students sound theology and zeal, despite his school's lack of conventional college resources.

Besides, if his students needed further training in a non-ecclesiastical subject like physics, they could enroll in another mentorship or school. In fact, one of William's students, John Redman, did just that, and later established such a successful career that it should have shut the mouths of Tennent's critics.

FATHER OF AMERICAN MEDICINE

If the Synod was so concerned about the limited opportunities that possibly awaited graduates from mentorships or unconventional colleges, their fears should have been laid to rest by the success of William's student John Redman. After Redman graduated from the Log College in 1744, he attended medical school and became a prominent doctor. Later he served on the first medical staff of America's first hospital (Pennsylvania Hospital), and became co-founder and first president of the College of Physicians (Philadelphia).

More notably, Dr. Redman mentored two of early America's foremost physicians: Dr. Benjamin Rush (signer of the Declaration of Independence and father of American psychiatry), and Dr. John Morgan (Physician-in-Chief of the American Continental Army and co-founder of America's first medical school). Therefore, if Dr. Redman was a founding father of American medicine, arguably his primary teacher—William Tennent—would be its grandfather!

According to the Examining Act, Dr. Redman's Log College education should have left him "marred" for the field of medicine, because he was not equipped by an approved school. Instead, Tennent skilled Redman in the language of medicine (Latin), and biblically shaped his worldview. Furthermore, Nathaniel Irwin, the third pastor of Tennent's Neshaminy church, wrote in 1793 how *several persons who became eminent in their secular profession received their education in arts and languages at this Academy* [the Log College]. *Distinguished among these stands Dr. John Redman.*"[65]

This shows that William did not exclusively equip people for the pulpit, but for community leadership. One professor of church history even believed Tennent's students surpassed their detractors both intellectually and morally. The Log College's curriculum more than adequately provided the foundational tools for the top three learned professions of their day: medicine, law, and most definitely the ministry.

CHAPTER SEVEN

DARKEST BEFORE
THE DAWN

Never confuse a single defeat with a final defeat.
—F. Scott Fitzgerald (1896-1940), writer[66]

On the surface, the Synod's Examining Act prevented "unqualified" men from getting a ministerial license. Everyone agreed that church leadership was a sacred trust, not meant for the incompetent or new converts (see I Timothy 3:6). Other leadership qualifiers were that they not be **"pugnacious"** or **"quarrelsome" (NIV)** (which some might think would disqualify Gilbert Tennent!), but be **"respectable," "gentle," (see I Timothy 2:2-3)** and skilled in **"accurately handling the word of truth" (see II Timothy 2:15).** The Presbyterian ministers, including the Tennents, also accepted the requirement for candidates to present either a diploma from an accredited university or evidence of being *"well skilled in the several branches of philosophy and divinity and the language."*[67] But the Tennents opposed the Act on the point of who was able to decide who was qualified for leadership.

THE SUBSCRIPTIONIST PARTY

In addition to insinuating the Log College was substandard to universities, the Act changed the screening process for ministry candidates. They used to be screened at the local level—by the presbyteries. Now, this Act elevated the screening to the Synod level. This would have been no issue except that the Subscriptionist Party controlled most of the presbyteries in the Synod.

The Subscriptionist ministers not only opposed the revivalists, but they stressed rigid conformity with all points of the creedal "Westminster Confession" as a test of faith. This was despite the fact that a number of the Synod's members disapproved of strict adherence to any human formula as a test of faith. Gilbert concluded that the Subscriptionists were:

> *induced to content themselves with a dead form of piety, resulting from a religious education, and historical faith; instead of seeking after the power and life of Christianity....*[68]

The lesson of the Subscriptionists is we should beware not to let our hearts deceive us into believing that intellectual assent to God's Word is the same as heart appropriation of its truths or of the Word Himself. In other words, knowing something intellectually is not the same as having something added to your life. When the Son of God rebuked the spiritual leader Nicodemus in John 3:10, the Greek rendition of Jesus' rebuke states that Nicodemus lacked an *experiential knowledge* of the New Birth. As Matthew Henry wrote,

It is possible for men to be very studious in the letter of the Scripture, and yet to be strangers to the power and influence of it.[69]

Thus endowed with this new political power, the Subscriptionist-dominated Synod could pack its membership with ministers they deemed compliant with their ministry standards. If this happened, it would jeopardize the very mission of the Log College—to fill the church with born-again, revival-friendly ministers.

Years later, the Synod wrote a revealing letter to Yale's president, stating that before the Examining Act was introduced, the presbyteries *"admitted to the ministry"* some of William Tennent's students, whom *"many of the Synod"* judged as not having *"sufficient qualifications."*[70] According to the Synod, *"those that were educated in this private way decried the usefulness of some parts of learning that we thought very necessary."*

The Subscriptionists believed any minister who disdained a "well-rounded" education greatly devalued the call to ministry. This is why the Synod, through these Acts, considered voting on *"tak[ing] all private schools where young men were educated for the ministry so far under their care...."*[71] This, feared the revivalists, would include the Log College itself. After much deliberation, the time for casting votes came. If the Synod voted to implement the controversial resolutions, the implications would be far-reaching.

To the consternation of the Tennents, *"a great majority"* of the members approved both Acts. The Subscriptionist-dominated Synod was now vested with the authority to screen out all "undesirable" applicants.

But an impassioned Gilbert Tennent refused to idly stand by while his father's school stood before this ecclesiastical firing squad. His family raised this ministry from its birth! It was the dream into which his father had poured his life for the past twelve years! No, Gilbert refused to keep silent. Voicing his objection to the vote, he *"cried out that this was to prevent his father's school for training gracious men for the ministry."*[72] To him there was much more at stake here than just the survival of his family's ministry project. The Examining and Itinerancy Acts, in a larger sense, signaled a declaration of war between the revivalists and Subscriptionists over who controlled the ministry.

Soon after the vote, the Synod appointed two screening committees. Surprisingly, to the northern committee were appointed Gilbert Tennent and Jonathan Dickinson, two men who would later co-labor to establish an advanced version of the Log College (now called Princeton University). Whereas to the southern committee, were appointed John Thomson and Francis Alison, two men who later led the opposition against the forthcoming Great Awakening.

OPEN DEFIANCE

According to Gilbert, the Log College sympathizers applied for the establishment of the New Brunswick Presbytery primarily to pack the Synod with born-again revivalists. If successful, the voting majority should shift in their favor. But because of the Examining Act, the Synod was now vested with full credentialing authority, and the New Brunswick Presbytery's intentions were curtailed.

When the New Brunswick Presbytery first met two months later (in August 1738), their first act of business was to examine Log College graduate, John Rowland, for the ministry. This was a blatant violation of the Examining Act. Gilbert Tennent's new presbytery argued that they *"were not in point of conscience restrained by said* [Examining] *Act from using the liberty and power which presbyter*[ies] *have all along hitherto enjoyed."*[73]

The following month the rebel presbytery issued Rowland a license to preach as an evangelist-at-large. Since the Synod majority ruled to accept the Examining and Itinerancy Acts, Gilbert's presbytery should have submitted, especially because these new procedures did not directly violate Scripture. But their defiance of the Synod only alienated them all the more.

As for "Hellfire" Rowland (as he was later called because he greatly stressed "the terrors"), he was originally denied licensure by the New Castle Presbytery because they considered him *"remarkably deficient in many parts of the useful learning required in our Directory,"* which was their book of church guidelines.[74] Even Rowland's mentor, William Tennent, expressed doubts about his protégé's competency, and recommended to the New Castle Presbytery that his student first fill his learning gaps at Francis Alison's school in New London, Pennsylvania. Nevertheless, Gilbert Tennent's New Brunswick Presbytery overlooked Rowland's record and licensed him anyway.

The Rowland episode grew more complex when a congregation within the bounds of the Philadelphia Presbytery petitioned the New Brunswick Presbytery for

Rowland to fill their pulpit, despite the *"irregularity of his licensing."*[75] A local minister, however, objected to Rowland's so-called intrusion, and therefore invoked the Itinerancy Act. Rowland ignored the warning, and the rest was inevitable.

Two weeks later, the Philadelphia Presbytery *"unanimously concluded they cannot accept Mr. Rowland as an orderly licensed preacher, nor approve of his preaching . . . until his way be cleared by complying with the order of Synod aforesaid."*[76] Sadly, William was absent from this presbytery meeting and was unable to defend his former pupil's reputation.

Moreover, during that same meeting, the Neshaminy faction reemerged to submit a petition signed by sixty-six of Tennent's church people, requesting the presbytery to provide other ministers to assist their aging pastor. Since William was absent, the presbytery decided to meet at Neshaminy the following month to settle the issue. (Interestingly, among those who presided over the faction's case was none other than the minister who first objected to Rowland's intrusion!)

The Scriptures say that whenever strife and disorder surface in relationships it is because someone has **"jealousy and selfish ambition"** in their heart (see James 3:16). William Tennent, therefore, had to proceed with humility and caution. The meeting at Neshaminy convened October 1738, where Tennent and his faithful congregants submitted to the presbytery court their reasons why the presbytery should not grant the faction's request for associate pastors.

As the proceedings continued, *"Mr. Tennent put an end to any more debate by freely and cheerfully agreeing to have an assistant, which was very satisfying to all parties and to the*

Presbytery."[77] Thankfully, the elder pastor did not choose the path of defiance that his zealous son Gilbert followed. Instead, he humbled himself to the wishes of the majority, and followed two scriptural admonitions:

> **The Lord's bond-servant *must not be quarrelsome*, but be kind to all, able to teach, *patient when wronged* (II Timothy 2:24).**

> **If possible, so far as it depends on you, be at peace with all men (Romans 12:18).**

But regrettably the Neshaminy issue was only temporarily resolved—and the worst was yet to come.

A YEAR OF SETBACKS

If William Tennent were asked when the lowest point of his ministry was, most certainly the year 1739 would come to his mind. Two formidable foes—the controversial Acts and the Neshaminy faction both paid him more unwelcome visits. But the most tragic of all for William was when death took his only daughter Eleanor at the age of thirty. The crises the Tennents faced that year must have tested their endurance to the utmost.

When the Synod met in the spring of 1739, the New Brunswick Presbytery (led by Gilbert Tennent) introduced their written objections to the controversial Acts:

1. They protested the power transfer from the presbyteries to the Synod.

2. They believed the Itinerancy Act obstructed the fulfillment of such biblical mandates as being

ready to preach **"in season and out of season" (see II Timothy 4:2),** and Paul's liberal attitude towards the gospel being preached in all places (see Philippians 1:15-19).

3. They felt the Itinerancy Act fostered suspicion among the ministers.

4. They concluded if the Synod passed those Acts because they wished to curb the potential spread of false doctrine, then *every* preacher should quit preaching since no man is perfect.

After the Synod members deliberated the above objections to the Acts, they drafted an even stricter addendum, stating now that *any* minister in *any* presbytery who objected to a certain minister's "intrusive" itinerancy could summon that itinerant before the Synod. This, argued the Synod, was to prevent *"unqualified men from creeping in among us...."*[78] In contrast, the Log College supporters believed the Act, especially with this new addendum, would greatly bog down the work of evangelism.

While a great majority of the Synod voted for the addendum, the Tennents, Samuel Blair, and five others dissented. Moreover, the Synod officially revoked "Hellfire" Rowland's ministry credentials, and encouraged all Presbyterians not to accept him as a preacher until he was licensed by the Synod. Furthermore, the Synod admonished the New Brunswick Presbytery for being *"very disorderly"* for using *"such divisive courses,"* such as licensing Rowland.[79] Again, a great majority voted in favor of the rebukes.

Interestingly, hours after the New Brunswick Presbytery was reprimanded, the Synod legislated to build *"a school or seminary of learning"* or *"college"* of its own.[80] What's more, it was passed unanimously, which means the Log College supporters voted for it despite their qualms over the Acts. For the moment, everyone's vision for equipping people for the ministry exceeded their party politics.

But according to the Synod, Gilbert also warned that *"he would oppose our design of getting assistance to erect a college wherever we* [the Synod] *should make application, and would maintain young men at his father's school in opposition to us."[81]* This, however, seems contradictory since Gilbert and the other Log College men voted in favor of building a Synod-operated college.

THE LAST STRAW

Initially, William Tennent cheerfully agreed to have an assistant pastor, until September 18, 1739, when a committee from the Philadelphia Presbytery came to Neshaminy to ordain Francis McHenry as his new assistant. This was the first time since Neshaminy's founding that William would regularly share his pulpit with another minister. But what made this more difficult for Tennent was that he had worked with McHenry before at the Newtown church, and knew he was sympathetic to the anti-revivalist Subscriptionists.

During McHenry's ordination ceremony, William probably tried to forget the church politics that brought this all about. Yet even on such a momentous occasion as this, the factional group reconvened their fight to remove their church's founder. It was hoped that McHenry's ordination would appease the church party. But as long as Tennent remained Neshaminy's pastor, his discontented parishioners determined to make his life miserable. Once again they filed a complaint—but this time their reason had merit.

The Philadelphia Presbytery was called to Neshaminy to preside over a new trial, and the charge was that Tennent allowed his former pupil Rowland—the very same whom the Synod defrocked—to preach at his church. When called to explain, Tennent not only *"justified the action"* but *"disclaim*[ed] *the authority of the presbytery to take cognizance of the matter...."* To accentuate his indignation, William *"contemptuously withdrew"* from the meeting and also from his presbytery.

Probably with much reluctance, Tennent's supporters sided with the committee's judgment that their pastor had acted *"disorderly and especially when aggravated by justifying of said action, and indecently withdrawing from the Presbytery."*[82] But William was not a man without a presbytery for too long. Four weeks later, the New Brunswick Presbytery invited him to join their ranks. But as to why William acted so indignantly before the committee and his own church people still remains a mystery.

Seeking reinforcement, the New Brunswick Presbytery wrote a letter to Jonathan Edwards, asking the famed New England revivalist to send revivalist candidates their way. But Edwards replied that he was in the same dilemma as they: revivalist candidates were as rare in New England as in the middle colonies. With William Tennent's health declining, and the Subscriptionists blocking the New Brunswick's recruiting and releasing of more revivalists, things looked bleak. The future of the Log College seemed uncertain.

ON THE HORIZON

Maybe it was no coincidence that the assaults against Tennent greatly intensified soon after he started the Log College. But why did he have to struggle so much when all he wanted was to do God's will and serve people? Even though he knew that **"our struggle is not against flesh and blood" (see Ephesians 6:12),** surely under this intense time of testing any person, including Tennent, would be tempted to reconsider their ministry call. But how much more testing could he endure?

Nobody likes to be misunderstood, let alone persecuted. However, all those who try to follow the Lord's will for their lives will face misunderstanding, persecution, and suffering at some point (see Philippians 1:29-30; II Timothy 3:12). It is a part of His curriculum to transform us into overcomers (see I John 5:5). Although Tennent was misunderstood and persecuted by his colleagues and church people, he, like Christ, **"learned obedience from the things which He suffered" (see Hebrews 5:8; Acts 26:19)** and determined to follow **"the heavenly vision"** that God placed in his heart.

Weary, perhaps, from all the power struggles, William Tennent sorted through the numerous questions swirling in his mind. Should he give his opponents the benefit of the doubt? Was God judging his ministry because he built it on wrong motives? Maybe the Synod ministers wanted the same end as he did—to see believers spiritually equipped—but only by different means. If true, maybe William and Gilbert were mistakenly reacting.

On the other hand, if his Synod colleagues had their way, then everything he had invested in the Log College—his time, his money, and his heart—would be lost. So did God want him to stand his ground and **"fight the good fight of faith"** for the Log College? **(see I Timothy 6:12)** Or, should he resign completely in order to keep peace?

Thankfully, things turned around just before that year (1739) came to a close. While ministers on all sides wrangled over church politics, God was about to pour out on their communities a great spiritual awakening that would surprise them all. Perhaps this explains what fueled much of the church power-struggles: Satan foresaw the coming move of God, and thus sent a preemptive strike to divide those Presbyterian ministers before the revival took effect. And perhaps this explains why God chose an outsider named George Whitefield to ignite the greatest spiritual revival to ever touch their shores.

Neshaminy-Warwick Presbyterian Church, founded and pastored by William Tennent Sr. in Warminster, Pennsylvania. (Used by permission.)

CHAPTER EIGHT

THE AWAKENING BEGINS

*When God in so remarkable a manner took the work
into His own hands, there was as much done in a day or
two, as at ordinary times...is done in a year.*
—*Jonathan Edwards*[83]

M ounting his horse, the gray haired William Tennent set off for Philadelphia, hoping that his errand would prove to be a divine connection. Perhaps the news of George Whitefield's recent arrival in the Quaker City came initially as a delightful diversion for the Log College headmaster. Albeit Whitefield was younger than William's youngest son, and something about him made the sixty-nine year old preacher overlook the generation gap.

This young Anglican priest was more than an evangelist—he was the most powerful revivalist America had ever seen. What's more, Whitefield epitomized everything for which William worked. If William could persuade the young celebrity to join efforts with the revivalists, it would be more than a match made in heaven. It would be the final step to unleash the greatest revival of the century.

ORIGIN OF THE AWAKENER

The story of Whitefield (pronounced "Whitfield") has fascinated people for almost three centuries, and rightly so. The supernatural anointing on his life was without comparison in his century. Even the great English actor David Garrick said Whitefield's preaching was so gripping he could bring an audience to tears just by mouthing the word "Mesopotamia." The Scottish philosopher David Hume (an agnostic) said it was worth traveling twenty miles to hear Whitefield preach.

Therefore, understanding Whitefield's relationship with the Tennents is essential to our story; for when he teamed up his ministry with theirs, the Log College men were catapulted to national influence. So where did Whitefield come from, and how did he acquire such a powerful anointing?

The twenty-four year old Whitefield overcame numerous obstacles years before becoming God's Great Awakener. For starters, he was badly cross-eyed, and his critics cruelly referred to him as "Dr. Squintum." He came from a poor family, leaving him to work his way through college (at Oxford). While at the university, the soul of the young Whitefield became *athirst for some spiritual friends to lift up my hands when they hung down, and to strengthen my feeble knees.* The cry of his heart was answered when he made *"one of the most profitable visits I ever made in my life"*—he befriended the famed Wesley brothers, John and Charles (founders of the Methodist church movement).[84]

The Wesleys took the young tavern-keeper's son under their wings, and gave him a treatise called *The Life of God in the Soul of Man* that forever changed his life:

> *Though I had fasted, watched and prayed, and received the [communion] sacrament so long, yet I never knew what true religion was, till God sent me that excellent treatise by the hands of my never-to-be-forgotten friend* [Charles Wesley].

The content of the treatise *"instantaneously darted"* his soul, and became the theme of his evangelistic ministry from thereon:

> *At my first reading it, I wondered what the author meant by saying, "That some falsely placed religion in going to church, doing hurt to no one, being constant in the duties of the closet, and now and then reaching out their hands to give alms to their poor neighbors."*

> *"Alas!" thought I, "if this be not true religion, what is?" God soon showed me; for in reading a few lines further, that "true religion was union of the soul with God, and Christ formed within us," a ray of Divine light was instantaneously darted in upon my soul, and from that moment, but not till then, did I know that I must be a new creature.*

When Whitefield told his relatives and friends *"there was such a thing as the new birth,"* they thought he was crazy. He then resolved to keep his revelation quiet, *"lest that, by any means the good work which God had begun in my soul might be made of none effect."*[85]

THE AWAKENER AWAKENED

In the meantime, Whitefield came under the tutelage of the Wesleys and soon adopted their "Methodist" religious lifestyle of living *"by rule and method."*[86] With a deep hunger to get closer to God, Whitefield would often go to the extreme and impose severe self-discipline. But then came the fateful day when Whitefield ceased his striving. Collapsing on his bed out of pure desperation and exhaustion, he cried out to God, *"I thirst! I thirst!"*

"Soon after this," Whitefield recalled, *"I found and felt in myself that I was delivered from the burden that had so heavily oppressed me...and I knew what it was truly to rejoice in God my Savior; and, for some time could not avoid singing psalms wherever I was."*

Whitefield had experienced the New Birth! As he put it, it was a time when:

[God] *enable*[d] *me to lay hold on His dear Son by a living faith, and by giving me the spirit of adoption, to seal me, as I humbly hope, even to the day of everlasting redemption. But oh! With what joy—joy unspeakable— even joy that was full of and big with glory was my soul filled when the weight of sin was laid off, and an abiding sense of the pardoning love of God, and a full assurance of faith broke in upon my disconsolate soul!*[87]

Whitefield learned that his born-again experience did not come through performing good works or assenting to Christian doctrine, but by surrendering his life to the One Who declared to all generations, **"Ye must be born again!" (see John 3:7 KJV)** This was the **"new and living** way" (see **Hebrews 10:20; II Corinthians 5:20**) that George read about in the Scriptures—not to require of people more religious activity or doctrinal purity, but to **"be reconciled to God."**

Burning with a newfound mission, Whitefield became convinced that "[t]*he Christian world is in a deep sleep! Nothing but a loud voice can awaken them out of it.*"[88] Initially, his message was not like "the terrors" of the Tennents. His was more of a compassionate plea, leaving him at times to break down in tears in the middle of his messages. One time, while crying before an audience, Whitefield said:

> *You blame me for weeping but how can I help it when you will not weep for yourselves, though your souls are upon the verge of destruction. And for aught I know, you are hearing your last sermon!*[89]

Although ordained an Anglican priest, Whitefield felt he was kin with anyone who shared with him the same born-again experience, regardless of their denominational affiliation. So when the young revivalist met William Tennent in November 1739, he postured himself not as "God's man of the hour," but as a humble disciple who wanted—and needed—to learn from others.

MEETING THE TEAM

Although Whitefield's goal for visiting the middle colonies was to raise funds for an orphanage he founded in Georgia, God had other plans for him. Because Whitefield knew God had a special purpose for his life, he felt compelled to document his travels for the sake of posterity.

Thankfully, one of those occasions was his eventful meeting with William Tennent. As it turned out, this was the first of many divine connections that awaited the young Anglican.

> *November 10, 1739 . . .* [W]*as much comforted by the coming of Mr. Tennent, an old grey-headed disciple and soldier of Jesus Christ. He keeps an academy twenty miles from Philadelphia . . . and, as far as I can find, both he and his sons are secretly despised by the generality of the Synod . . . Returned home* [from preaching at a prison] *with the Swedish minister and old Mr. Tennent. Conversed with them of the things of God. . . .*

Then, a few days later in New Brunswick, Whitefield found himself a mentor, who happened to be born the same year as his friend John Wesley—the son of the *"grey-headed disciple"* he had just met.

> *Here we were much refreshed with the company of Mr. Gilbert Tennent, an eminent Dissenting minister, about forty years of age, son of that good old man who came to see me on Saturday at Philadelphia. God, I find, has been pleased greatly to own his labors. He and his associates are now burning and shining lights of this part of America . . .* [P]*reached in the evening at Mr. Tennent's meeting house. . . .*

How magnanimous it was of Gilbert to let this young priest of the Established Church, whom he barely knew, preach in his Presbyterian church. The next day, Whitefield found himself a new traveling associate.

> *Set out from Brunswick, in company with my dear fellow-travelers, and my worthy brother and fellow laborer,*

Mr. Tennent. As we passed along, we spent our time most agreeably in telling one another what God has done for our souls. He recounted to me many instances of God's striving with his heart and how grace, at last, overcame all his fightings against God.[90]

Then came that humbling moment in New York when George saw a side of Gilbert that deeply affected him:

Then I went to the meeting-house to hear Mr. Gilbert Tennent preach, and never before heard such a searching sermon. He convinced me more and more that we can preach the Gospel of Christ no further than we have experienced the power of it in our own hearts. Being deeply convicted of sin, by God's Holy Spirit, at his first conversion, he has learned experimentally [i.e., experientially] *to dissect the heart of a natural man.... He is a son of thunder, and does not fear the faces of men.*

After sermon, we spent the evening together at Mr. Noble's house. My soul was humbled and melted down with a sense of God's mercies, and I found more and more what a babe and novice I was in the things of God.[91]

SEEKING BALANCE

Less than a week later, Whitefield was introduced to the man whom God would use to take the Log College vision to its next level—Jonathan Dickinson. Although Dickinson was renowned for his sagacity and sense of balance, he was not a convinced supporter of the revivals, at first. Just three weeks before Whitefield landed in October, Dickinson sought to resolve the Synod's controversies between the Tennent sympathizers and the Subscriptionists through his pamphlet, *Danger of Schisms and Contentions*. If the Subscriptionists and revivalists both heeded Dickinson's message, they would have saved themselves and others much pain in the ensuing years.

Dickinson addressed in his sermon-pamphlet the issue of unfairly judging ministers based on their gifts or lack thereof:

> *Must one minister be vilified and condemned because God has given superior gifts and graces to another? Must Paul be despised on account of Apollos' eloquence of speech? Or Apollos be contemptuously treated because Paul exceeded him in all the extraordinary gifts of the Spirit? . . . Are all Sons of Thunder? No!* **"God set the members every one of them in the body, as it hath pleased him"** *(I Corinthians 12:18 KJV). And we are accordingly to esteem and value all that are carefully discharging the awful trust committed to them of the Lord,* **"as ministers of Christ and stewards of the mysteries of the kingdom"** *(I Corinthians 4:1).*

Then Dickinson, in a roundabout way, addressed the issue of ministers rashly judging people's born-again experience, which both the Subscriptionists and revivalists accused each other of doing:

> *Shall we "limit the holy one of Israel"? Or confine the operations of divine grace to any special or particular methods? Doesn't continual observance convince us that the Spirit of God does in a variety of ways, means, and*

degrees awaken sinners to a sense of their guilt and danger; and bring them from a state of carnal security to the footstool of His mercy?[92]

A month after writing his *Schisms* sermon, Dickinson invited Whitefield to preach in his church to seven hundred people. Unashamedly, Whitefield preached *"against both ministers and people among the Dissenters, who hold the truth in unrighteousness, contenting themselves with a bare, speculative knowledge of the doctrines of grace, but never experiencing the power of them in their hearts."*[93]

REVIVAL AT NESHAMINY

After his visit with Dickinson, Whitefield returned to Gilbert's church to preach to *"a large assembly gathered together from all parts."* Here he met Gilbert's other mentor, that *"worthy old soldier of Jesus Christ,"* Frelinghuysen, and the following day he met "Hellfire" Rowland.[94] It was as if God was introducing Whitefield to His American revivalist team! Then Whitefield paid a historic visit to "the place where you drink twice"—Neshaminy:

Nov. 22, 1739—Set out for Neshaminy . . . where old Mr. Tennent lives, and keeps an academy, and where I was to preach today, according to appointment. We came thither about twelve, and found above three thousand people gathered together in the meeting-house yard; and Mr. William Tennent preaching to them, because we were beyond the appointed time.

When I came up, he soon stopped, and sang a psalm, and then I began to speak. At first the people seemed unaffected, but in the midst of my discourse, the hearers began to be melted down, and cried much. After I had finished, Mr. Gilbert Tennent gave a word of exhortation.

Then Whitefield recorded for posterity a scene from the life of the Tennent household.

After our exercises were over, we went to old Mr. Tennent, who entertained us like one of the ancient patriarchs. His wife to me seemed like Elizabeth and he like Zacharias. Both, as far as I can find, walk in all the ordinances and commandments of the Lord blameless. We had sweet communion with each other, and spent the evening in concerting measures for promoting our Lord's kingdom.

During his Neshaminy visit, Whitefield was shown the fountainhead of American Presbyterian revivalism—the Log College. It was also at this time he learned of the Tennents' plan for founding the New Brunswick Presbytery:

It happens very providentially, that Mr. Tennent and his Brethren are appointed to be a presbytery by the Synod, so that they intend breeding up gracious youths, and sending them out into our Lord's vineyard.

The place wherein the young men study now is in contempt called "the College." It is a log-house, about twenty feet long, and nearly as many broad; and, to me, it seemed to resemble the schools of the old prophets. That their habitations were mean [meager], and that they sought not great things for themselves, is plain from the passage of Scripture....

Whitefield's *"schools of the old prophets"* comparison refers to the equipping schools headed by Old Testament prophets, Samuel and Elisha. Whitefield continued his commentary on Tennent's school:

> *From this despised place, seven or eight worthy ministers of Jesus have lately been sent forth; more are almost ready to be sent; and a foundation is now being laid for the instruction of many others. The devil will certainly rage against them, but the work, I am persuaded, is of God, and will not come to naught.*
>
> *Carnal ministers oppose them strongly; and because people, when awakened by Mr. Tennent or his brethren, see through them, and therefore leave their ministry, the poor gentlemen are loaded with contempt, and looked upon as persons that turn the world upside down.*

The next day, Whitefield departed from *"dear Mr. Tennent, and his other worthy fellow-laborers, but promised to remember each other publicly in our prayers."* [95]

SPIRITUAL WARFARE

In a letter Whitefield wrote to William Tennent a couple of months later, he included such an extraordinary prayer for Tennent, that if every one of us likewise prayed this prayer for each other, who knows how dramatically different the church of Jesus Christ would be:

> *Oh that you may experience fresh anointings and teaching from above! O that you may be strengthened by God's mighty power in the inner man, and pull down Satan's strongholds daily.* [96]

Whitefield rightly discerned that William's fight for the Log College was not a war "**...against flesh and blood, but against the rulers, against the powers, against the world forces of this darkness, against the spiritual forces of wickedness in the heavenly places" (Ephesians 6:12).** Although a number of colonial clergy thought they were doing God's work by opposing the Log College (see John 16:2), the revivalists needed to remember that their fight was not against people, but against demonic powers which sought to enslave people through mental strongholds of lies and faulty ideas.

When Whitefield revisited Neshaminy, his associate William Seward chronicled the visit:

> *Had sweet converse with old Mr. Tennent and his spouse, and with their young disciples of Jesus Christ. O what a slur did this cast on all human learning when a little log house has produced more godly ministers within these ten years, than both the universities of Oxford and Cambridge, excepting those of our Brother Whitefield and Wesley's [Methodist] Society.*
>
> *Whitefield and I gave each of us something towards the support of this Seminary, which may justly be called a School of the Prophets. I doubt not, if our polite students were to come see them, they would look on them as a parcel of poor idiots.*[97]

This was a classic case of the Lord choosing the despised to confound the wise (see I Corinthians 1:27-28). What is more, Whitefield and Seward had enough vision to invest in this work while it was still in its infancy.

KINDRED SPIRITS

Although Gilbert was ten years Whitefield's senior, the two were kindred spirits. This especially is evident in an emotional letter Gilbert wrote to Whitefield about a week after his Anglican brother in Christ visited the Log College:

> *I think I never found such a strong and passionate affection to any stranger as to you* [Whitefield], *when I saw your courage and labor for God at New York. I found a willingness in my heart to die with you, or to die for you. I thought if a spear was pointed at your bosom I could willingly have received the thrust to prevent your death... The reason why I spoke so little for the most part of the time while I was with you was a shameful sense I had of my ignorance and barrenness.*
>
> *Since you were here, I have been among my own people* [in New Brunswick] *dealing with them plainly about their soul's state in their houses, examining them one by one as to their experiences, and telling natural people the danger of their state; and exhorting them that they were totally secure, to seek convictions, and those that were convinced to seek Jesus; and reproving pious people for their faults.*

When someone like Gilbert has a "kingdom of God" perspective instead of a "my kingdom" or "my ministry" perspective, they are not threatened by other people emerging or surpassing them. They have a heart like John the Baptist, who had great influence in all Israel and Judea, yet selflessly decreased his ministry while Another (Jesus) increased His.

Then Gilbert closed his letter to Whitefield by mentioning how he prayed for *"the private academies of our friends in Scotland and England . . . And at my father's* [school]*, that God would prosper them, and incline his people to support them."* [98]

OUTSIDE THEIR CIRCLES

Though occasionally the Tennent brothers and several Log College alumni teamed up to spread the New Birth message, they also humbled themselves to learn from and work with like-visionaries outside their denominational circle, such as Whitefield (Anglican), Frelinghuysen (Dutch-Reformed), and Jonathan Edwards (Congregationalist). Because Jesus Christ was their common denominator, these men cared not who **"planted the seed,"** or who **"watered it,"** just as long as **"God made it grow" (see I Corinthians 3:6 NIV).** They just wanted to see, as Whitefield put it, *"a revival of true and undefiled religion in all sects whatsoever!"* [99]

Another school planter with whom they collaborated was German-Reformed minister, Peter Henry Dorsius. Interestingly, Dorsius, who is the founder of American ministerial education in the German-Reformed denomination, was also neighbor to William Tennent. He arrived in the Neshaminy area in the fall of 1737 to pastor a church during the time when William struggled with the factional group. One of Dorsius' students, John Henry Goetschius, became second only to Frelinghuysen in promoting the Awakening among the Dutch settlers.

Soon after Gilbert Tennent and Frelinghuysen examined Goetschius for the ministry, they and Dorsius unlawfully ordained Goetschius, when ordinations were only to be performed back in Europe. Later, Frelinghuysen's son and Goetschius became known for their work in helping found Queens College (now Rutgers University) in New Jersey. Interestingly, part of the founding vision for Rutgers was *"that it may be a school of the prophets in which young Levites and Nazarites of God may be prepared to enter upon the sacred ministerial office in the church of God."[100]*

The Great Awakening was a time when the mainline denominations birthed during Europe's Reformation were experiencing another reformation, namely in the areas of ministry training and ordination.

But what of William Tennent's place in the Great Awakening? Most see him in a supporting role and not a principal character. However, in God's economy, whether someone works on the frontline or supports the line, the faithful are all rewarded their fair share (see I Samuel 30:24-25; Matthew 20:12-16). Although Tennent was not directly involved in converting the masses, through his sacrificial **"labor of love" (see I Thessalonians 1:3)** he equipped many to evangelize and equip the masses. Gilbert praised his father's endeavor this way:

> *Whatever contempt these men . . . are pleased to cast upon the* [Log College] *school under my honored father's tuition; yet multitudes of pious people in this land can witness that divers who have come out of it have been eminently successful in propagating the truly noble interests of vital Christianity.*
>
> *As the design of its instruction was to introduce more faithful ministers into the church, that thereby*

experimental and practical religion might, together with human learning, be promoted, so it has pleased a gracious God (adored be His name) to crown with auspicious smiles the humble essays [endeavors] *that have been made to serve His glory and His church.*[101]

CHAPTER NINE
SURVIVAL AMIDST REVIVAL

Must we leave off every duty that is the occasion of
contention or division? Then we must quit powerful
religion altogether....
—*Gilbert Tennent*[102]

When the Great Awakening first started in America, most may have thought it would be a passing whim, not realizing it would ebb and flow for almost thirty years! During its height in 1740, entire communities reportedly repented of their sins. Large audiences flocked to hear the Tennents, Whitefield, Rowland, and Blair preach their revival messages. Ben Franklin, for instance, reported in his *Pennsylvania Gazette* some effects the revival had on society:

> *The alteration in the face of religion here* [in Philadelphia] *is altogether surprising . . . religion is become the subject of most conversations. Instead of idle songs and ballads, the people are everywhere entertaining themselves with psalms, hymns, and spiritual songs.*[103]

Franklin also noted in his famous autobiography how shocked he was by the spiritual climate change in Philadelphia because of a recent Whitefield meeting:

The multitudes of all sects and denominations that attended his sermons were enormous . . . It was wonderful to see the change soon made in the manners of our inhabitants. From being thoughtless and indifferent about religion, it seemed as if all the world were growing religious, so that one could not walk through the town in an evening without hearing psalms sung in different families of every street . . . I computed that he might well be heard by more than thirty thousand. This reconciled me to the newspaper accounts of his having preached to twenty-five thousand people in the fields....[104]

A SON OF THUNDER

As for Gilbert Tennent, a nineteenth century historian observed that his popularity in America was second only to Whitefield's during the Great Awakening. New England pastor Thomas Prince (1687-1758), publisher of the *Christian History* newspaper, wrote a lengthy profile of Gilbert that is worth reading:

He [Gilbert] *seemed to have no regard to please the eyes of his hearers with agreeable gesture, nor their ears with delivery, nor their fancy with language; but to aim directly at their hearts and consciences, to lay open the ruinous delusions, show them their numerous, secret, hypocritical shifts in religion, and drive them out of every deceitful refuge wherein they made themselves easy with the form of godliness without the power.*

And many who were pleased in a good conceit of themselves before, now found, to their great distress, they were only self-deceived hypocrites. And though, while the discovery was making some at first raged, as they have owned to me and others, yet in the progress of the discovery many were forced to submit; and then the power of God so broke and humbled them, that they wanted a further and even a thorough discovery; they went to hear him, that the secret corruptions and delusions of their hearts might be more discovered; and the more searching the sermon, the more acceptable it was to their anxious minds.

Then Prince turned his focus on Gilbert's ministry style:

As to Mr. Tennent's preaching: It was frequently both terrible and searching. It was often for matter justly terrible, as he, according to the inspired oracles, exhibited the dreadful holiness, justice, law, threatenings, truth, power, majesty of God; and His anger with rebellious, impenitent, unbelieving, and Christless sinners; the awful danger they were every moment in of being struck down to hell, and being damned forever; with the amazing miseries of that place of torment....

Such were the convictions wrought in many hundreds in this town by Mr. Tennent's searching ministry . . . And indeed by all their converse I found, it was not so much the terror as the searching nature of his ministry, that was the principal means of their conviction. [105]

Some may question the benefits of the *"searching nature"* of Gilbert's ministry, but as Matthew Henry aptly put it, *"Sinners own consciences are reformers' best friends."* [106] One

Boston minister reported that ever since Gilbert and Whitefield toured New England three months earlier, six hundred people had come to him for help because they were under deep spiritual conviction. Another minister reported over a thousand such cases coming to him.

On one occasion, Gilbert's preaching at Yale College impacted a student named David Brainerd who later became known for his mission work among the American Indians. Furthermore, Brainerd's famous diary (edited by Jonathan Edwards) continues to inspire many to enter the mission field.

BY THEIR FRUITS

The thousands who heard Whitefield and the Log College students found messages delivered with an inspiration rarely heard before. In communities that experienced a mass conversion, it was rare for an unconverted person to be in their midst. What God did in the Great Awakening, and through the Log College revivalists and others, altered the course of America for the better. Just imagine how different America would be if those revivals never brought about these changes:

- The revivals helped release the colonies from the inordinate hold of England's mother church, and thus made the political break inevitable.

- They prepared the Colonists religiously for the trials of the American Revolution.

- They greatly increased mission work among the Indians.

- They propagated American-born education through the founding of such colleges and universities as Princeton, Pennsylvania, Rutgers, Brown, and Dartmouth.

- They cultivated religious freedom and tolerance, which helped dissolve barriers between denominations, communities, and classes.

- They increased the value of the common man, which opened the door for the creation of America's democratic-republic form of government.

- They fostered anti-slavery sentiments among some of the Colonists.

However, more important than all of these changes is that thousands of people, due to the move of God and the efforts of the revivalists, experienced Christ's New Birth!

UNCONVERTED MINISTRIES?

But not all were happy with William Tennent's students. The turning point came in March 1740, when Gilbert Tennent preached his provocative sermon: *The Danger of an Unconverted Ministry*. With the brazenness of an Old Testament prophet, Gilbert pronounced the work of unconverted ministers as counterproductive to the work of Christ, sapping the very life of the church instead of bringing it life.

Is it reasonable to suppose that they [unconverted ministers] *will be earnestly concerned for others' salvation when they slight their own? Our Lord reproved Nicodemus for taking upon himself the office of instructing others while he himself was a stranger to the New Birth (see John 3:3).*

...These foolish builders do but strengthen men's carnal security by their soft, selfish, cowardly discourses. They do not have the courage or honesty to thrust the nail of terror into sleeping souls.

...Is a blind man fit to be a guide in a very dangerous way? Is a dead man fit to bring others to life? A mad man fit to give to cast out devils? A rebel, an enemy to God, fit to be sent on an embassy of peace to bring rebels into a state of friendship with God? A captive bound in the massy chains of darkness and guilt, a proper person to set others at liberty?

...Is an ignorant rustic that has never been at sea in his life fit to be a pilot, to keep vessels from being dashed to pieces upon rocks and sand-banks? Isn't an unconverted minister like a man who would teach others to swim before he has learned it himself, and so is drowned in the act and dies like a fool?

...Pharisee-teachers will, with the utmost hate, oppose the very work of God's Spirit upon the souls of men, and labor by all means to blacken it as well as the Instruments...Thus did the Pharisees deal with our Savior.

The most practical solution to this unconverted ministry crisis, Gilbert asserted, was for Christians to implement the Log College model. Planting schools of the prophets, where people could be effectively equipped for their callings, was the most viable means for pulling the lethargic body of Christ out of its miry quandary. Gilbert continued:

> *The most likely method to stock a church with a faithful ministry, in the present situation of things, the public academies being so much corrupted and abused generally, is to encourage private schools or seminaries of learning, which are under the care of skillful and experienced Christians; in which those only should be admitted who, upon strict examination have, in the judgment of a reasonable charity, the plain evidences of experimental* [i.e., experiential] *religion.*
>
> *Pious and experienced youths who have a good natural capacity, and great desires after ministerial work, from good motives, might be sought for, and found up and down in the country, and put to private Schools of the prophets, especially in such places where the public ones are not.*
>
> *This method, in my opinion, has a notable tendency. It builds up the church for the coming of His Kingdom. The church should be ready, according to their ability, to give something, from time to time, for the support of such poor youths who have nothing of their own. . .Oh! If the love of God is in you, it will constrain you to do something to promote so noble and necessary a work.*

Gilbert also charged churchgoers as accomplices in the church's demise, because they tolerated, and sometimes preferred, ministers who were not *"harping upon terror, and sounding damnation in our ears...."* No doubt the grave words of the Apostle Paul must have come to Gilbert's mind:

**For the time will come when they will not
endure sound doctrine; but *wanting to have their
ears tickled,* they will accumulate for themselves
teachers in accordance to their own desires (II
Timothy 4:3).**

ATTACKING TERRITORIALISM

Gilbert then turned his attack on the centuries-old
mindset of religious territorialism, which believes that
people should not freely visit other churches, and ministers
should not "infringe" on another minister's territory.

*If God's people have a right to the gifts of all God's
ministers, pray, why may they not use them as they have
opportunity? And, if they should go a few miles farther
than ordinary to enjoy those which they profit most by,
who do they wrong? Now, our Lord informs His people
that whether Paul, or Apollos, or Cephas, all was theirs
(see I Corinthians 3:22).*

*...Besides, it is an unscriptural infringement on
Christian liberty (see I Corinthians 3:22). If the great ends
of hearing may be attained as well, and better, by hearing
another minister than our own, then I see not why
we should be under a fatal necessity of hearing. . .our
parish-minister, perpetually or generally. Now, what are,
or ought to be, the ends of hearing but the getting of grace
and growing in it? (see Romans 10:14)*

*...Faith is said to come by hearing (see Romans 10).
But the apostle doesn't add 'your parish-minister.' Isn't
the same Word preached out[side] of our parish? And is*

there any restriction in the promises of blessing the Word to those only who keep within their parish-line ordinarily?

...I have known persons to get saving good to their souls by hearing over their parish-line; and this makes me earnest in defense of it. . .Now if it is lawful to withdraw from the ministry of a pious man in the case aforesaid, how much more from the ministry of a natural man?

Gilbert here was attempting to raise his listeners' understanding of what constitutes the church of Jesus Christ—a question that theologians have wrangled with for centuries. The revivalists (and particularly Whitefield) knew that Christ's church could never be fully represented by only one arm of the visible church. It transcends any one congregation, denomination, or movement.

This is why the Log College men collaborated with, and even befriended, ministers outside of their church circles. They believed in tolerating people's *non-essential* religious preferences, as long as those preferences did not cheapen or contradict a gospel essential. (The gospel essentials include Christ's full divinity and humanity; the divine authority of the Scriptures; living free from sin; etc.) Acquiring and maintaining this nonsectarian perspective of Christ's church requires a teachable heart—a willingness to learn from other Christians outside of our church circle.

As for the revivalists, because they tried to maintain a nonsectarian spirit without compromising the gospel essentials, God used them to string together the isolated strands of revival in colonial America. (For an enlightening study on handling the non-essentials of Christianity, read the Apostle Paul's exposition on liberty of conscience in Romans Chapter 14.)

ORDER AND DIVISION

To preempt any hostility his *Unconverted* message might incite, Gilbert exhorted his hearers to always expect *"opposition and division"* anywhere *"true religion"* is advanced:

> *Pray, must we leave off every duty that is the occasion of contention or division? Then we must quit powerful religion altogether, for "he that will live godly in Christ Jesus will suffer persecution." And particularly, we must carefully avoid faithful preaching, for that is wont to occasion disturbances and divisions, especially when accompanied by Divine power (see I Thessalonians 1:5-6). "Our gospel came not unto you in word only, but in power;" and then it is added that they "received the word in much affliction."*
>
> *...It is true, the power of the gospel is not the proper cause of those divisions, but the innocent occasion only. No, the proper and selfish lusts are the proper cause of those divisions. And very often natural men, who are the proper causes of the divisions aforesaid, are wont to deal with God's servants as Potiphar's wife did by Joseph; they lay all the blame of their own wickedness at their doors, and make a loud cry!*[107]

Gilbert's analogy of Potiphar's wife so accurately depicts those who practice religious territorialism—they quickly blame others instead of examining themselves before the Lord. Religious territorialism is rooted in the two primary enemies of the cross—pride and fear.

Territorialism sets in when we inordinately take ownership of what God has only given to us to steward for Him. This is pride—to think more highly of ourselves than we ought (see Romans 12:3). When someone has territorial tendencies (whether they be clergy or layperson), they see anything that conflicts with their wishes as a threat to their control—which gives place to fear.

For those of us who battle territorialism or control, Solomon gave us an enlightening proverb worth meditating on: **"Where no oxen are, the manger is clean, but much revenue comes by the strength of the ox" (Proverbs 14:4).** We all prefer to have a proverbial "clean manger," whether it comes in the form of a clean and orderly home life, workplace, or church meeting. But is our primary goal to have a "clean manger" or to have an "ox" that the manger was designed for?

What if the Lord calls us to a work that will "mess up" our current lifestyles? Surely the Tennents, especially in their advanced years, would have preferred not to go through the trouble of building a log school in their backyard or to regularly cook for and clean after their ministers-in-training. But how willing are we to sacrifice our manageable "clean manger" for the strength—and the mess—of the "ox" that God may have for us?

Sadly, many of us who want God to release another Great Awakening want its benefits, but are unwilling to endure the "messy manger" which typically accompanies it. In His parable of the wheat and the tares (weeds), Jesus said for the sake of the "wheat" we should let the wheat and tares grow together until they both mature, and then *let Him* do the separating (see Matthew 13:24-30; 36-43). Instead of our focusing on keeping our fields "weed-free" or our "mangers" clean, let us seek the Lord for:

1. the patience of Gamaliel, who cautioned his overzealous and misguided colleagues to not act rashly (see Acts 5:34-41);

2. the discernment of Paul, who admonished us to examine everything and extract the good from the bad (see I Thessalonians 5:19-21).

SUPPORTING LOG COLLEGES

Sadly, Gilbert's inflammatory remarks against the spiritual deadness and error in the Christian church overpowered his plea for planting and supporting equipping schools. But there were some—like the Nottingham church (where he delivered his *Unconverted* message)—who dared to take up his challenge. When Log College alumnus Samuel Finley took the pastorate of Nottingham four years later (in 1744), he founded the Nottingham Academy, which still operates to this day. In fact, some leading Americans who sat personally under Finley's tutelage there went on to perform great accomplishments:

- Two signed the Declaration of Independence (Richard Stockton and Finley's nephew, Dr. Benjamin Rush);

- Two became state governors;

- Nine became college founders, including Dr. Rush who founded Dickinson College;

- One became the first U.S. postmaster general;

- Three became surgeon generals of the Revolutionary Army;

- Nine became physicians;

- And sixteen became ministers.

Moreover, two of Finley's students, John Morgan and William Shippen, co-founded the University of Pennsylvania Medical School, and awarded the first medical diplomas in America to two other Finley students, John Archer and James Tilton. Again, just as with Log College graduate Dr. John Redman, we see another connection between William Tennent and the founding of America's medical establishment.

The New Brunswick Presbytery heeded Gilbert's call for more log colleges by supporting *"some students at Neshaminy"* that were *"in need of assistance."*[108] Even Whitefield donated *"towards the support of this* [Log College] *Seminary,"* trusting that *"the Lord will increase it, as he did the little lad's loaves and fishes."*[109] Likewise, Log College graduates Charles McKnight and William Tennent, Jr. founded a school in Lower Freehold, New Jersey. Months after Gilbert's sermon, the New Londonderry (Faggs Manor) Church, pastored by Log College alumnus Samuel Blair, also caught the vision, founded a school, and financially supported *"several very promising and hopeful youths under the care and instruction of the Rev. Mr. Tennent at Neshaminy...."*[110]

Like those colonial visionaries, we need to pray that the Lord would grant us the opportunity to make financial provision now for the equipping of His people. Just as King David donated much of his treasure for the future building of the Lord's temple (which he never lived to see, I

Chronicles 29:2), let us pray that God would grant us **"an abundance for every good deed" (see II Corinthians 9:8).**

NEGATIVE REACTION

But not everyone supported Gilbert's idea to plant more log colleges. For instance, Reverend John Hancock, grandfather of the first signer of the Declaration of Independence, circulated two pamphlets against Gilbert, entitled *The Danger of an Unqualified Ministry* and *The Examiner or Gilbert Against Tennent*. In the latter, Hancock asserted how *"it's generally thought"* that if Gilbert's proposal for proliferating log colleges *"was built upon the ruin of our public academies, neither religion nor learning would be greatly served thereby."* Hancock further insinuated that Gilbert's motive for proposing more log colleges was his way of validating *"his father's log-house."*[111]

Gilbert countered Hancock with a poignant pamphlet called, *The Examiner Examined, or Gilbert Tennent Harmonious*:

> *What if the proposal* [for multiplying log colleges] *had a favorable aspect upon the* [Neshaminy] *log-house, where is the harm of it? May not persons be taught as well in a log-house as in a stone or brick house? In the meantime, every eye may see that the proposal respects not one house more than another where both piety and learning are more regarded.*

Gilbert further argued that:

> *The insinuation of building the log house upon the ruin of public academies is invidious and without*

*foundation . . . The distance between this private school
and any public academies is so great that there is no danger
of its interfering with them.*[112]

But even if the schools were within the same vicinity,
why not have more schools? Does not history teach us that
where market competition exists quality will surface? It
seems Hancock's attack on Gilbert was motivated more by
territorialism than by reason.

Then on June 1, 1741 the tensions erupted between
what were called the "Old Side" Subscriptionists in the Synod
and the "New Side" revival supporters. ("Old Side" refers to
those who sided with the old Synod of Philadelphia, and the
"New Side" to those who sided with Gilbert's New Brunswick
Presbytery and the more revival-friendly new Synod of New
York, which formed later.) Although Gilbert's New Side
Presbytery *"differed with our brethren* [in the Synod] *in respect
to some acts and canons they had made,"* the New Siders still
"designed no separation" from the Synod. But the
Subscriptionists had had enough of the revivalists, claiming
they were anarchical and schismatic. Therefore, the
Subscriptionists submitted to the Synod an official protest
against their revival colleagues *"to sit as members of this Synod."*[114]

Conversely, the revivalists had enough of the
Subscriptionists. After unsuccessfully protesting the
Subscriptionists' protest, the Tennent group felt forced to
withdraw from the Synod. Sadly, the breach between the
Old and New Sides remained unhealed for seventeen years.
The Log College men were now a presbytery without a Synod.

Over the next four years, however, the New Brunswick
Presbytery worked to align with other revival-friendly

presbyteries, and eventually confederated into a new Synod (the Synod of New York). Shortly after, the Log College graduates also had the satisfaction of seeing an advanced version of their alma mater planted just across the Pennsylvania line in New Jersey (as discussed in the next chapter). But sadly, their teacher William Tennent never got to share in the joy.

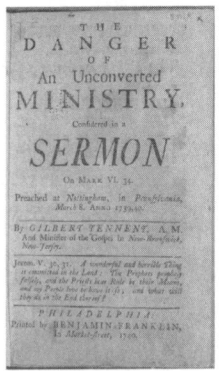

Gilbert Tennent's controversial pamphlet, "The Danger Of An Unconverted Ministry," printed by Benjamin Franklin. It contributed to the splitting of the American Presbyterian denomination.

CHAPTER TEN

CHANGING OF
THE GUARD

Though our great intention was to erect a seminary for educating ministers of the gospel, yet we hope it will be useful in other learned professions—Ornaments of the State as well as the Church.

—Aaron Burr, Sr. (1716-1757), co-founder of Princeton University[115]

Sensing the end was near, William commenced with drafting his will:

This Sixteenth day of February, Anno Domini One thousand, Seven hundred and Forty-five, I, William Tennent Senior, minister of the Gospel in the Township of Warminister in the County of Bucks and Province of Pennsylvania, being weak in body but of sound mind and memory, thanks be to God, therefore call to mind the mortality of my body, and knowing that it is appointed for all once to die, do make and ordain this my last Will and Testament....[116]

For the last three years, the aging William set his house in order. Because of *"his inability by reason of advanced age to discharge the work of the ministry,"* William retired from his Neshaminy pastorate on May 29, 1742.[117] He hoped the New Brunswick Presbytery would provide ministers for Neshaminy who would build and not destroy the foundation he had laid. To his relief, they selected such men as his former pupil, William Robinson, and a local New Side pastor, Richard Treat, to fill in whenever possible. But above all, William had to trust that God **"...is able to guard what I have entrusted to Him until that day" (II Timothy 1:12).**

UNLESS A GRAIN DIES

Nineteen months later (December 1743), William saw the reins of the Neshaminy work pass to his former student Charles Beatty. With a large assembly witnessing Beatty's ordination, William's son, Gilbert, delivered a fitting message entitled, *"Love to Christ a Necessary Qualification in Order to Feed His Sheep."*

But months before Beatty's ordination, the Old Side-New Side tensions that stewed among the Neshaminy congregation finally reached their boiling point. Old Side parishioners disputed with New Siders over who were the rightful owners of the church's property. Francis McHenry, Tennent's former assistant pastor, sided with the Old Side, while Beatty sided with the New.

Although the New Siders stood in the majority, they acquiesced their legal rights and built *"a more large and more elegant"* building just a stone's throw away from the original.[118] And there the rivaling churches remained at odds for fourteen years. (Today the Neshaminy congregation resides in the New Side's building.) William Tennent, however, never lived long enough to see his church nor his denomination reunite.

From the time Tennent retired, at least five more Log College students were released into the ministry: John Roan (1742); William's successor, Charles Beatty (1742); Dr. John Redman (1742); Daniel Lawrence (1745); and John Campbell (1746). For a season, William allowed his former student, John Roan, to manage his college. Then four months after retiring, William put his homestead and his Log College up for sale. But for reasons unknown, his property remained unsold until shortly after his death.

Then on May 6, 1746, William Tennent slipped into eternity at the ripe age of seventy-three. His body was laid to rest in Neshaminy's cemetery, where a table stone was placed over his grave with this inscription:

Here lyeth the body of the
Rev. Mr. William Tennent, Sen:
who departed this life May the 6: Anno Dom:
1746 Annos Natus 73.
"Ashes to Ashes, Dust to Dust"
But the memory of his life
And the inspiration of his teaching
Will endure as long as time shall last.
Founder of the Log College,
Founder of Neshaminy Church, 1724
First church erected in 1727-28

Years later, a granite memorial was placed over his grave with this fitting epitaph:

In Memory of
Rev. William Tennent, Sen.
Pastor of Neshaminy Church 1726-1742
And Deep Run Church 1726-1738
Died May 6, 1746 aged 73 years
Founder of the Log College
Struxit Melius Quam Scivet★
★"He built better than he knew"

As one early biographer wrote of Tennent:

Some men accomplish much more by those whom they educate than by their own personal labor . . . They [the Log College] *had, we have reason to believe, the teaching of the Holy Spirit, and without the advantages which others enjoyed, they became "burning and shining lights."*[119]

After William's death, Catherine Tennent sold the homestead and moved to Philadelphia to live with her son Gilbert. There she remained until her dying day on May 7, 1753, the day after the seventh anniversary of her beloved William's death.

But what became of William's Log College? The new owners of the Tennent plantation were ignorant of the significance of their purchase. According to William's son Charles, the owners converted the rustic revival school into a pigsty. It was as if this precious pearl of ministry training was figuratively cast before swine! Today, a large ministry called Christ's Home for Children owns the Log College property. The only known remains of the Log College, however, are a piece of wood donated to Princeton Theological Seminary by one of William's descendants, and an early nineteenth century walking stick made from one of its logs.

But why did not one of William's sons, students, or the New Side Neshaminy Church keep the Log College going? Why did God allow the school to die with its founder? The only clue to this mystery is found in these words of Jesus: **"Truly, truly, I say to you, unless a grain of wheat falls into the earth and dies, it remains alone; but if it dies, it bears much fruit" (John 12:24).** Just as Abraham offered up his son Isaac, and God offered up His Son Jesus, God oftentimes lets His purposes experience a death so He can raise them up with greater life and power.

When the Log College forever closed its doors upon William's death, its legacy experienced a momentary death, until a year later when it was resurrected just across the Delaware River. During the final year of William's life, in the colony of New Jersey, plans were laid for perpetuating his vision for a revival-friendly school of higher learning. In fact, embedded in the corporate seal of this new school would be the image of an open Bible with the Latin motto above it: "Vitam Mortuis Reddo" (*"I restore life to the dead"*). No, Tennent's "school of the prophets" did not remain dead. Instead, it was resurrected, and it would then bear greater fruit.

CHANGING OF THE GUARD

The setting for the origin of the advanced version of the Log College was during the heat of the Old Side-New Side conflicts. Some revival-friendly ministers such as Jonathan Dickinson and Aaron Burr, Sr. discerned, as Tennent did years earlier, the critical need to equip people with Christ-centered higher education. Moreover, they grew troubled over Harvard and Yale's anti-revival stance, and especially Yale's bigotry against student and future famed missionary, David Brainerd.

But Dickinson's associates were also dissatisfied with the Log College's limited training. These visionaries realized not everyone was called strictly to pulpit ministry. As Burr put it:

> *Though our great intention was to erect a seminary for educating ministers of the gospel, yet we hope it will be useful in other learned professions—Ornaments of the State as well as the Church. Therefore we plan to make the plan of education as extensive as our circumstances will admit.* [120]

In other words, they envisioned building a Christian institution that would train people not exclusively for church ministry, but for those God was calling to work in the fields of science, politics, education, and law.

In March 1745, a year before Tennent died, Dickinson and Burr, key leaders in the New York Presbytery, began raising funds for their advanced version of the Log College. In the tradition of William Tennent, they sought to establish it in Dickinson's home in Elizabeth, New Jersey. However, their first major roadblock surfaced when New Jersey's royal governor, a man hostile to anything non-Anglican, rejected their request to charter a school.

All seemed hopeless, until the royal governor died three weeks after Tennent's death. Taking advantage of the timing, Dickinson and his associates petitioned the acting governor for a charter. To avoid any more roadblocks, they worded their petition to comply with the charter of New

Jersey, which promised religious freedom. In October 1746, only five months after the Log College folded, these New Siders were granted their request to open their school, naming it The College of New Jersey (one-hundred fifty years later, it was renamed Princeton University).

Soon after, Dickinson recruited Log College alumni Gilbert and William Tennent, Jr., Samuel Blair, and Samuel Finley among its first trustees. Three weeks after the first anniversary of William Tennent's death, the new school commenced in Dickinson's home, with about ten students attending, and Dickinson acting as its first president. Even though the new college was primarily Presbyterian, its founders envisioned it to be all-inclusive, where *"persons of all persuasions are to have free access to the honors and privileges of the College, while they behave themselves with sobriety and virtue."*[121]

Woven into the school's fabric would be the nonsectarian spirit of the Great Awakening, with *"equal liberties and privileges secured to every denomination of Christians."*[122] In keeping with this spirit, the faculty bestowed honorary degrees on non-Presbyterian revivalists Frelinghuysen and Whitefield. The New Jersey College was becoming a school with the academic excellence of the New England universities, and the spirit of the more-tempered revivalists.

MORE SCHOOLS BORN

The College of New Jersey was not the only collegiate planted during the Great Awakening period. What is known today as the University of Pennsylvania, for instance, began when supporters of Whitefield erected a *"house of public worship"* and a charity school where *"useful literature and the knowledge of the Christian religion"* were taught.[123] By the next decade, the Whitefield church broke away from the school, and elected Gilbert Tennent as its pastor. The school quickly enlarged to a university, thanks to the patronage of Ben Franklin and others.

Soon after, universities such as Dartmouth, Rutgers, Columbia, and Brown sprang up, all with the intent of evangelizing and training people for the ministry. For instance, Columbia University, originally called King's College, declared in its founding charter: *"The chief thing that is aimed at in this college is to teach the children to know God in Jesus Christ...."*[124]

And what about the Old Siders? Did they ever build a school of their own? Not really. In 1744, the Synod took oversight of an existing school—the New London Academy, which was near Log College alumnus Samuel Blair's school in Faggs Manor. However, when the Synod requested an endorsement for their school by Yale's president, Yale not only refused to help, but the New London Academy's headmaster later resigned to accept the rectorship of the University of Pennsylvania. After a few changes in the Academy's leadership, the school eventually relocated to the colony of Delaware, where it grew into the University of Delaware.

THE PRINCETON CONNECTION

To be accurate, the Log College was not the direct predecessor of Princeton University, but rather its precursor. It is plausible that Dickinson and his co-founders, who were all Harvard and Yale graduates, *"first concocted the plan and foundation of the College*" back during the explosive 1739 meeting when the Synod proposed "*erecting a school or seminary of learning.*"[125] In response, the Synod appointed Dickinson and a man named Ebenezer Pemberton (who later co-founded the College of New Jersey with Dickinson) to raise funds in Europe for the Synod's school, but nothing apparently came of the venture.

But in 1745, while William Tennent waited out his final months, these two men, along with Aaron Burr, led the way for their New York Presbytery to pull out of the Synod to join the Log College-dominated New Brunswick Presbytery. And also during this time, their interest in establishing a school of their own began to materialize.

Soon after Dickinson's college was chartered in 1746, the Log College men began filling its ranks. As mentioned, four of the first twelve trustees of the school were students of William Tennent. Later, graduates John Blair, Charles Beatty, and Dr. John Redman were added. Then, Gilbert Tennent and Samuel Davies (a graduate of Blair's log school, and later fourth president of the College of New Jersey) were appointed fundraisers for the construction of the school's first building, Nassau Hall. Their soliciting message for the college was: "*as religion ought to be the end of all instruction . . . one of the primary views of this foundation was to educate young gentlemen for the sacred office of the ministry and fit them for the discharge of so noble an employment....*"[126]

GILBERT, THE RECONCILER

During his overseas fundraising trip, Gilbert's provocative *Unconverted Ministry* sermon (which Ben Franklin later published) returned to haunt him. When some Old Siders circulated his sermon in the United Kingdom, it created quite a stir among Gilbert's potential patrons. Thankfully, he regained his credibility by giving them the conciliatory *The Peace of Jerusalem* sermon-pamphlet he had published a few years before.

In his *Peace* pamphlet, Gilbert publicly apologized to both the Old and New Side Synods for the judgmental tone of his *Unconverted Ministry* message. Furthermore, he emphasized the need for love to balance out the extremes of the Subscriptionists' stoicism and the revivalists' zealotry. As Matthew Henry wrote decades before Gilbert learned his lesson:

> *Discretion must always guide and govern our zeal, that we do nothing unbecoming ourselves, or mischievous to others.*[127]

In fact, years later Gilbert published his last sermon-pamphlet called *Nature of Religious Zeal Explained*, in which he shared the proper place for emotions and reason:

> *Light [reason] and heat [emotions] are inseparable companions to religion, without the latter the former is cold formality; and without the former the latter is wild enthusiasm....*[128]

As Christ said, true devotion to Him will always include our emotions and our intelligence, our hearts and our minds (see Matthew 22:37).

As for us, how can we prevent ourselves from taking anything spiritual to an extreme? For starters, we must realize that from time to time, we all tend to see things in extremes. We all have misjudged people and events based on our limited knowledge and wounded emotions. In addition to studying the Bible, the key safeguards to our living between extremes are walking in Christ's humility and love. Consequently, when we cultivate His humility and love in our hearts, His wisdom will inevitably come (see Proverbs 11:2; 8:1). Then, with these three virtues in hand—humility, love, and godly wisdom—we can safely stay within biblical parameters.

Although Gilbert did not have a *"change of sentiment about the late revival of religion,"* he wanted a *"compromising of the matters of difference"* between the two parties and to *"promote peace and union in the best manner I can."* Yet to foster reconciliation, Gilbert catalogued the values that both parties held in common, such as:

> [The] *nature and necessity of conversion to God as it is held forth in the Scriptures, and in our* [Westminster] *Confession of Faith . . . in church discipline (in all essentials) as represented in the Holy Scriptures, and in our Directory* [of church order].

Their only differences, he qualified, were based *"entirely upon circumstantials . . . or as the inspired Apostle phrases, the matters of 'doubtful disputation' (see Romans 14:1 KJV)."*[129] Needless to say, his *Peace* pamphlet greatly appeased not only his potential college patrons, but also his Old Side colleagues.

As a final point regarding Princeton's connection with William Tennent's school, Whitefield himself verified in 1756 that the Log College *"is now increased to a large college, now erecting in the New Jerseys. May it increase with all the increase of God.* "[130] In the main entryway of Princeton's Nassau Hall, hangs a copper plaque that tells of the Ivy League's roots stemming back to Tennent's Neshaminy School.

Although during its early years the fledgling New Jersey College equipped leading figures in American history, it did not come without a price. And part of that price was paid with the untimely deaths of most of its first five presidents.

The gravesite of William Tennent, Sr. in Warminster,
Pennsylvania. Engraved in Latin atop the gravestone is written:
"He built better than he knew."
(Used by permission.)

CHAPTER ELEVEN

ENLARGING THE VISION

"I sent you to reap that for which you have not labored; others have labored, and you have entered into their labor" (John 4:38).

During its first two decades, the College of New Jersey experienced significant strides and tragedies. On the day after its first anniversary, the infant school's first president, Jonathan Dickinson, died leaving Dickinson's youthful partner Aaron Burr, Sr. (father of the future Vice-President of the United States) to retrieve the fallen presidential mantle. Due to Burr's leadership, the school developed a collegiate quality about it, establishing entrance exams, a set curriculum, rules and regulations, and a new campus in the small town of Princeton. However, his success is not measured as much by the organization he brought to the school, but by the success of those he equipped.

EQUIPPING AMERICA'S FOUNDERS

It has been said, *"It is only as we develop others that we permanently succeed."*[131] With this in mind, here is a list of the leaders that graduated from the College of New Jersey during Burr's ten-year presidency:

- Sixty-two ministers, two of whom founded Dartmouth College and Washington and Lee University;

- Six lawyers, two of whom were state chief justices; one "President" of colonial Pennsylvania; and one U.S. Senator;

- One state governor (North Carolina);

- Eight physicians, two of which founded America's first and second oldest medical schools;

- Several teachers and businessmen, one of which became mayor of New York City, and another high sheriff of London, England.

Tragically, a year after the College moved to the village of Princeton (1757), the overextended Burr fell ill and died at the young age of forty-one. Five days later, the trustees elected his father-in-law, Jonathan Edwards, to assume the presidency. Edwards was an excellent choice—a prominent revivalist and the most eminent philosopher-theologian in the country.

Initially, Edwards turned down their presidential offer out of concern for his health, feeling the job would distract him from his writing ministry. Additionally, he had conducted mission work among the Indians ever since his church dismissed him years earlier. A year later the reluctant revivalist reconsidered and accepted the New Jersey College's offer. But within two months of his taking office, Edwards died from a smallpox inoculation. In Gilbert's obituary on Edwards, he had published the final moments of the New England revivalist's life on earth:

> *...he* [Edwards] *looked about, and said, "Now where is Jesus of Nazareth, my true and never failing Friend?" And so he fell asleep, and went to that Lord he loved.*[132]

SERVE YOUR GENERATION

After Edwards' unexpected death, the next choice for president was Samuel Davies, a graduate of the Log College's daughter school in Faggs Manor, superintended by Samuel Blair. Prior to accepting the presidency, Davies was renowned for pastoring the Hanover Revival, and later for greatly influencing the famed revolutionary Patrick Henry. One of the College's trustees remarked about Davies, "[T]*here was never a college happier in a president.*"[133] But everyone's happiness was short-lived, for eighteen months after assuming office Davies died at age thirty-eight, making him the third president to pass away within two years. To the graduating class of 1760, Davies left these memorable words:

> *Whatever be your place, imbibe and cherish a public spirit. Serve your generation. Live not for yourselves, but the public. Be servants of the church; the servants of your country; the servants of all.*[134]

Although Davies' term was brief, the fruit of his college work was great. From among the class of 1760 came these leaders:

- A number of Continental Army chaplains;
- A founder of a North Carolina college;

- A member of the U.S. House of Representatives;
- A signer of the Declaration of Independence.

After Davies' passing, Log College alumnus and Nottingham Academy founder Samuel Finley assumed the presidency, serving for five years until his death. Interestingly, the first three presidents of the New Jersey College were university trained, while the latter two were log-school trained, lacking formal degrees. Finley, however, received an honorary degree from the University of Glasgow, making him the second American minister endowed with such an honor. Noteworthy of the one hundred thirty students who graduated under Finley's term were:

- The founder of Brown University (converted under Gilbert Tennent);

- A governor of and first senator for New Jersey;

- A chief justice of the United States.

When Finley died, the school's vice president and Log College alumnus, John Blair (brother of Samuel Blair) became acting-president until the next president took office. By its twentieth anniversary, the College of New Jersey equipped almost half of its graduates as New Side ministers.

Before the close of the century, the College of New Jersey's staff carried William Tennent's vision of church renewal and ministry-training reform not only to the churches of America, but also to the very seats of civil government. For instance, nine of the fifty-five delegates to the Constitutional Convention in 1787 were graduates of the College of New Jersey. Under its sixth president,

John Witherspoon (who was the only minister to sign the Declaration of Independence, and to be a member of the Continental Congress during the entire Revolutionary War), the College of New Jersey equipped:

- One hundred fourteen students who became ministers;
- Thirteen who became state governors;
- Thirty-three who became U.S. Congressmen;
- Twenty who became U.S. Senators;
- Three who became Supreme Court Justices;
- One who became U.S. Vice-President (Aaron Burr, Jr.);
- And one who became the "father" of the U.S. Constitution, and later a U.S. President (James Madison).

William Tennent would have been pleased with the harvest produced by the College of New Jersey under its first six presidents. But when the seventh took office, the college's fruitful harvest began to spoil.

THE TURBULENT YEARS

It is one thing when trouble comes from the outside, but it is quite another when it erupts from within. The sight of Princeton's illustrious Nassau Hall set on fire by radical students (in 1807), was indelibly burned into President Samuel Smith's mind. Five years later, another riot broke out on the campus, leaving Smith to suspend one hundred twenty-five students, and almost his entire faculty! Later that year, Smith was forced to resign, and his entire religion department broke away to form its own ministry school (called Princeton Theological Seminary). So what brought the College of New Jersey—the heir of William Tennent's legacy—almost to the point of ruin?

When Smith assumed the presidency around the turn of the nineteenth century, America was under a great moral transition. Riding high on the victories of America's independence and the French Revolution's humanistic ideals, the rising generation enthusiastically sought to exercise their inalienable rights. People were infatuated with secularism and science, and grew cynical of organized religion. As one historian put it, most Americans saw themselves as *"masters of nature and her laws,"* and *"free beings who had no further need of the tutelage of church and state...."*[135]

Only twenty years before the Revolutionary War, however, the president of Yale wrote, *"Colleges are societies of ministers for training up persons for the work of the ministry."*[136] But from the commencement of the war until 1815, Yale College graduated only nine ministry candidates. That is one ministry candidate for every six years over a forty-year period! Ministers were once the spiritual and intellectual leaders of their communities, but now they found their social standing replaced by men of politics, science, and commerce.

Yet even in the midst of all this cultural change, reports circulated about revivals breaking out in the southern states and in New England's prestigious Ivy League—Yale.

ANOTHER GREAT AWAKENING

"If one generation begins to decline," wrote an early vice president of Harvard, *"the next that follows usually grows*

worse, and so on, till God pours out His Spirit again upon them.[137] While humanist activists were seeking to steer the Americans further away from God and His kingdom purposes, God was pouring out His Spirit on places like Yale College and the frontiers of Kentucky during what was coined the Second Great Awakening (1794-1804).

The primary vessel of the New England revival was Yale's president, Timothy Dwight, a grandson of Jonathan Edwards. Dwight attacked the Unitarian-Universalism doctrine that pervaded local churches and schools, such as Harvard. Under Dwight's administration, half of Yale's student body converted to Christ.

Spearheading the Kentucky revivals were two men with spiritual roots in the Log College movement: James McGready and Barton Stone. McGready was the key leader of the Logan County Revival (1800), and Stone of the Cane Ridge Revival (August 1801), where twenty-three thousand people attended.

Although McGready was mentored by an alumnus of Blair's Faggs Manor School, Stone and he attended the legendary Guilford log school near Greensboro, North Carolina. Before the Revolutionary War, the Guilford Academy was the center of education for the South. And not only did its founder, David Caldwell, have roots reaching back to Tennent's Log College, his very life patterned much of William Tennent's.

THE SOUTHERN LOG COLLEGE

David Caldwell (1725-1824) attended a log school in Pequea, Pennsylvania, operated by Robert Smith, an alumnus of Blair's Faggs Manor School. Caldwell then studied under Davies and Finley at the College of New Jersey, where after graduating, he returned to teach the classical languages. Later, Caldwell was licensed to preach by the Tennent-sponsored New Brunswick Presbytery, and like William Tennent, he took up farming to supplement his church income.

At the age of forty, Caldwell opened his legendary academy in his home. Again, like Tennent, Caldwell's teaching resources were very limited. A former student recalled:

> There was no library attached to [the school]. [Caldwell's] *students were supplied with a few of the Greek and Latin classics, Euclid's elements of mathematics, and Martin's Natural Philosophy. Moral philosophy was taught from a syllabus of lectures delivered by Dr. Witherspoon in Princeton College. The students had no books on history or miscellaneous literature.*

Nevertheless, Caldwell mentored three thousand students over his lifetime, despite the lack of resources. Five of his graduates, became state governors and more became U.S. Congressmen. Moreover, in the fifty-six years Caldwell ran his log school, *"frequent times of revival"* occurred.[138] A friend of Caldwell's mentioned how *"nearly all the young men who came into the ministry of the Presbyterian Church, for many years, not only in North Carolina, but in the states south and west of it, were trained in his school."*[139] In 1794, Caldwell was offered the first presidency of the newly formed University of North Carolina, which he declined due to his advanced age. Again, God used men with "Log College vision" to affect America.

THE SCHOOL MOVEMENT

One lesser-known fact about the Second Great Awakening is that its revivalists surpassed their predecessors by planting over six hundred schools. After these revivals abated, a great demand for ministers to evangelize the frontier ensued. But schools such as the College of New Jersey (under President Samuel Smith's administration) found themselves unable to meet that demand.

With the success of seminaries such as Andover, some of Princeton's leadership soon saw the seminary model as a plausible answer to their dilemma. In 1812, the year President Smith resigned, some of Princeton's leaders established Princeton Theological Seminary as a postgraduate ministry training school.

Much like the origins of the Log College and the College of New Jersey, the new Princeton seminary commenced with only one teacher—Archibald Alexander, who also wrote a definitive biography of William Tennent's Log College. Interestingly, a few of the Seminary's founders (according to Alexander) were *"strongly in favor of placing it on the very site of the Log College."*[140] Nathaniel Irwin, the third pastor of Tennent's Neshaminy church and Tennent's first biographer, designated in his will for $1,000 (or $13,754 in today's dollars) to be granted to the Seminary only if it was built upon the original site of the Log College—which never happened.

Many envisioned the new seminary would create greater freedom and focus to equip people. Interestingly, its founding vision was reminiscent of Dickinson and the Log College men's mission:

to unite in those who shall sustain the ministerial office. . . .piety of the heart, which is the fruit only of the renewing and sanctifying grace of God, with solid learning; believing that religion without learning, or learning without religion, in the ministers of the gospel, must ultimately prove injurious to the church.[141]

Although over the next two decades a crop of twenty-two new seminaries sprang up, the secularism of the day retaliated with the planting of its own schools of higher learning. Business tycoons such as John D. Rockefeller (oil), James Duke (tobacco), Ezra Cornell (telegraph and banking), Johns Hopkins (banking and railroads), and Leland Stanford (railroads) began subsidizing the formation of "modern" universities.

One secular textbook on education stated that *"reformers in the common-school movement,"* such as Horace Mann, an espoused Unitarian and architect of the American public school system, *"viewed parochial* [private religious] *schools as the greatest possible threat to democracy."*

In their minds, the goals of a common-school—moral training, discipline, patriotism, mutual understanding, formal equality, and cultural assimilation—could not be achieved if substantial numbers of children were in independent schools.[142]

Interestingly, this is the same territorial argument John Hancock made when attacking Gilbert's proposal for multiplying log schools. In this case, however, the territorialism was manifesting through the secular schools, which contended for the control of moral training.

THE BATTLE

This was a battle for the hearts and minds of people, and the arena was the classroom. As Abraham Lincoln presumably wrote, *"The philosophy of the school room in one generation will be the philosophy of the government in the next."*[143] In other words, whoever controlled the classroom gained the advantage for controlling the next generation. The great reformer Martin Luther wrote:

> *Every institution that does not unceasingly pursue the study of God's Word becomes corrupt... I greatly fear that the universities, unless they teach the Holy Scriptures diligently and impress them on the young students, are wide gates to hell.*[144]

For this reason, William Tennent started his Log College: to raise up leaders to change the church to change the world. Many of the Log College revivalists faithfully carried the mantle of their mentor with great success. But as time went on, their successors grew to value scholasticism over what the Apostle John described as **"His anointing [which] teaches you about all things, and is true" (see I John 2:27).** Thus, the descendants of the Log College exchanged the revivalist anointing for clerical professionalism. And their neglect became our loss. Yet for those who yearn to participate in God's purposes as Tennent did, it will take the resolve of Tennent to successfully carry the leadership mantle of **"equipping the saints" (see Ephesians 4:12).**

If you share the same burden as Tennent—to see people empowered and equipped by God's Spirit—the challenge may seem daunting. However, God does not require us to be successful according to the world's standards of success, but to be faithful to what He requires of us (see Matthew 25:21; II Corinthians 2:14). With this said, please prayerfully read the final chapter to see how the Lord may want you to also help change the church to change the world.

CHAPTER TWELVE

RECOVERING THE FIRE

*O God, send us the Holy Ghost! Give us both the breath
of spiritual life and the fire of unconquerable zeal . . .
God, send us a season of glorious disorder…Oh, for the
fire to fall again—fire which shall affect the most stolid!
Break down every barrier that hinders the incoming of
Thy might! Give us now both hearts of flame and
tongues of fire to preach Thy reconciling word, for Jesus'
sake! Amen!*

–Charles Spurgeon (1834-1892)[145]

William Tennent was an agent of change, and his vision should not be isolated to a certain time or place. Although Tennent, like David of old, **"served the purpose of God in his own generation" (see Acts 13:36)**, God's intention for Tennent's vision still remains unfinished. Early America sorely needed Tennent's equipping ministry to raise up revivalist church leaders. But as one Presbyterian seminary president observed, what is sorely needed today is for the church to *"shift from our present predominantly 'clerical paradigm' to a 'people of God paradigm.'"*[146]

The challenge of our century is to expand Tennent's equipping model by raising up revivalist laypeople—where born-again blue-collar workers, white-collar workers, teenagers, senior citizens, stay-at-home parents, and children are released as Spirit-empowered revivalists to fulfill the Great Commission (see Matthew 28:19-20).

Sadly, many continue to believe the unbiblical idea that ministry work is mainly for a certain "qualified" few. But as one Bible school president said, *"It is only through a fully trained laity that the world will be won to Christ."*[147] The Bible clearly states that *every* Christian is called to work in His ministry (see Ephesians 4:12; I Peter 2:9). The question is to what work is He calling each of us to fulfill?

Most people wrongly assume that the word "ministry" is synonymous with church work. Although the Lord does call some to full-time church-related jobs, this is not the biblical norm. He longs to manifest **"through us the sweet aroma of the knowledge of Him in every place" (see II Corinthians 2:14).** It is His strategic purpose to place people who are empowered by His Spirit in all segments of society—our school systems, our business communities, our government institutions, and our neighborhoods (see Luke 24:45-49; Acts 1:8; II Corinthians 5:20). And this will only happen when laypeople are clothed with the power, love, and self-discipline of His Holy Spirit (see II Timothy 1:7; Acts 2:1-4, 37-39; 18:25-26; 19:1-7; Romans 12:11).

RELEASING THE LAITY

Although much in the field of Christian education has improved over the years, this one challenge still lies before us: How can believers in the local church be released into their **"work of service"**? **(see Ephesians 4:12)** Frank Tillapaugh, a Baptist pastor and author, described the vicious circle which many churches fall into regarding the equipping issue:

Have you ever stopped to think about the built-in fallacy in the way we prepare people for leadership in churches? As students, they go to school in a fortress environment. For years, they spend much of their time in classrooms and libraries. The assumption is that if they hear the lectures and read the books they will be equipped to be leaders in the church. The reward system is built on grades....

After several years of this, they are asked to take a position in a church. Functionally, the church bears little resemblance to the school. The school-trained leader assumes that the way you equip people to live the Christian life is to give them a lot of facts about the Christian faith. You can't test the people, but you can surely lecture them ... If dumping content on people produced mature Christians, the church in the United States would be by far the most mature church which history has ever seen....

There is nothing wrong with what the schools are doing; it is just that we expect too much of them. Most are not in the position to provide the practical training needed. Perhaps this means we ought to expect more of the local church in preparing candidates for leadership.[148]

So within the context of a local church, what is the relationship between leaders and laity supposed to be? Leaders are to function as Spirit-led trainers who help believers grow into the image of the Savior. That is to say they are to coach God's players from the sidelines, while the Holy Spirit coaches the players personally out on the field (see Ephesians 4:11-12). Maybe this is why many Christians get frustrated and bored in their Christian walk—they are unnecessarily sitting on the bench, so to speak. Maybe all they need is for someone to pull them aside, as Priscilla and Aquila did in the Bible to a revivalist named Apollos, and explain to them **"the way of God more accurately" (see Acts 18:24-28).**

When Paul wrote that we should *"consider how to stimulate* **one another to love and good deeds" (see Hebrews 10:24),** he did not imply that church leaders alone were responsible for motivating believers to do the work God is stirring them to do. Again, Tillapaugh put it this way:

> *It is sad to see pastors trying to motivate their people with fear, ought-to, or you'll-be-blessed motivations. God uses want-to motivation, because that is the only kind of driving force which works for any length of time. . . The Holy Spirit working within directs us where He wants us to go, and He often uses want-to motivation to do so.*[149]

When Paul wrote that **"it is God who is at work in you, both to will and to work for His good pleasure" (see Philippians 2:13),** the phrase **"at work"** is the Greek word *"energeo,"* meaning "to energize." How encouraging it is to know that God energizes us *to want* to do His work!

Therefore, it is the responsibility of mature believers, whether they are officially in leadership or not, to help others identify the work which the Holy Spirit is energizing them to accomplish. This can be done by asking the person leading questions, such as:

- What are you passionate about in life?
- If you had the money, time, and training, what would you like to be doing right now?
- Have you prayed about what God is calling you to do with your life?

Then, let the mature believer spiritually discern the person's answers, realizing that oftentimes **"the answer of the tongue is from the Lord" (see Proverbs 16:1).** In other words, the person may surprisingly find their answer coming right out of their mouth, simply because someone else was there to lovingly draw it out of them.

EQUIPPING IDEAS

So what is it that people need to grow into their calling and gifting? Here are three key ingredients that must be included in any equipping process. To leave out any one of these three will only stunt people's growth:

- People need opportunity
- People need freedom
- People need encouragement

To help people step into what God is leading them to do, they must be offered growth opportunities that can strengthen their weaknesses and maximize their strengths. But opportunity alone is not enough. People must also feel they are free to take risks, to make mistakes, to be creative, and to share their dreams and fears.

In order to feel free, people must have someone in their life who encourages them, who lovingly gives them constructive feedback and assistance. And, above all, that Someone is the Lord Jesus, who "**...has granted to us *everything* pertaining to life and godliness, through the true knowledge of Him who called us by His own glory and excellence" (II Peter 1:3**).

On a more practical level, here are some ideas on how local congregations can help people grow into **"the work to which I** [the Lord] **have called them" (see Acts 13:2)**:

• *Vision-cast ministry opportunities.* Church leaders should make public any ministry opportunities the Lord places on their hearts, and then watch and wait for those who feel impelled to respond by stepping forward. This does not mean leaders have to be directly involved in every opportunity they present. All they need to do is sow the opportunity "seed," and let the Holy Spirit germinate it in people's hearts. For who knows if one door of opportunity may open for someone else a world of possibilities?

• *Start a mentorship, a home group, a marketplace Bible study, or a school, where people can meet with God and get equipped.* The goal of each of these group meetings is to manage them as Ahimelech managed the sanctuary in I Samuel 21. In this story, David ran to the sanctuary hungry and empty-handed. But thanks to Ahimelech's flexibility and hospitality, the future king left there with his arms laden with **"the bread of the Presence" (see I Samuel 21:6)** and the sword of his past victory—the sword of Goliath. Likewise, schools and small groups should be a place of flexibility and hospitality where the hungry and defenseless can come for nourishment and equipment. Small groups should be safe places for people to practice their ministry gifts, build relationships, and get constructive feedback, so they can grow into what God has called them to do.

• *Offer classes on how to be led by the Spirit of God.* The ultimate act of worship that any Christian can offer to their Lord is to learn to walk by the Spirit. The Bible says, **"For all who are being led by the Spirit of God, these are sons of God" (Romans 8:14).** What greater satisfaction can there be than to help train people to better recognize and follow the voice of their Shepherd? How differently would our homes, workplaces, neighborhoods, and churches be if we all learned to **"walk by the Spirit"?** **(see Galatians 5:25)** [For a practical resource regarding this subject please read *Surprised by the Voice of God*, by Dr. Jack Deere (Zondervan Publishing House).]

If, however, no ministry opportunity seems to be presenting itself in your life, why not do what William Tennent did and expand on what you are already doing? As one German proverb goes, *"Begin to weave and God will give you the thread."* That is, start with what you already have, regardless of what resources you may lack—people, equipment, finances, sufficient vision—and see what God does.

In Matthew 15:33-34, Christ's disciples rationalized that they lacked the necessary resources to meet the demands of the hour. But the Lord sought to turn their focus away from the natural to heaven's never-ending supply. Likewise, whenever we find ourselves lacking resources, we must realize that our adequacy only comes **"from God, who also made us adequate as servants of the new covenant..." (II Corinthians 3:5-6)**. And it is He who **"...will supply all your needs according to His riches in glory in Christ Jesus" (Philippians 4:19)**. So, let us begin to "weave" in faith, and watch how God will give us "the thread."

RECOVERING THE FIRE

' Conducting practical training, however, was only a part of William Tennent's equipping model. The key that turned his generation around was his training and releasing *revivalists* into the mission field. In other words, what distinguished Tennent's vision from conventional training methods was his stressing "revivalism"—the intense emphasis on personal religious experience, holy living, and the priesthood of all believers.

Sadly, although many school and church leaders covet the fruit of revivalism—such as rapid church growth—not many seem eager to incorporate revival theology into their core values. Since other authors have already explored the reasons why some people resist revivalism, I do not wish to duplicate their efforts at this time. Rather, I wish to speak to those who are discontented with the spiritual state of their personal lives, their churches, their jobs, and their schools—and are willing to do something about it.

Tennent could have tolerated the lack of revivalist training, the complacency of his fellow citizens, and the disregard for the New Birth by his clerical colleagues. However, something inside him refused to accept the status quo. To not change, in fact, would have proven more costly for him than to change. It has been said, *"We can't solve problems by using the same kind of thinking we used when we created them."*[150] Therefore, for those of us who wish to see things change, let us begin by asking the Lord how He wants to change us!

As the revivalists understood, and as Jesus graphically explained in Revelation 3:16-17, lukewarmness is the greatest enemy which every believer should vigilantly guard against. Lukewarmness—that attitudinal state of being **"neither hot nor cold"** for Christ—sets in when we stop hungering for God, or start hungering for other things more than God (verse 16). It leaves its victims with a false sense of feeling **"wealthy"** (superior) or in **"need of nothing"** (self-sufficiency or self-satisfaction) (verse 17). Those who are lukewarm proudly deceive themselves into believing they have no needs. They may believe in the need for revival, but not for themselves—that is beneath them.

THE REVIVALIST SECRET

Hunger for God, on the other hand, is what set Tennent's revivalists apart from others. Those men desperately needed God to send a Great Awakening to them—the kind where

He brings a **"demonstration of the Spirit and of power"** (**see I Corinthians 2:4-5**) and **"everyone** [keeps] **feeling a sense of awe"** (**see Acts 2:43**). If we will, likewise, keep in our hearts a **"sense of awe"** about the things of God, and obey Jesus' command to the lukewarm church—to **"be zealous and repent"** (**see Revelation 3:19**) (to keep our hearts passionate and contrite)—then we can avoid becoming that lamentable **"generation that did not prepare its heart and whose spirit was not faithful to God"** (**see Psalms 78:8**).

The greatest gift that God can give any human being is a hunger for Himself. Although we can **"kindle afresh the gift of God which is in you,"** as Paul told Timothy, our hunger for Him cannot be manufactured independently of Him (see II Timothy 1:6). It takes God to make us hungry for God (see John 6:44; 12:32). And the more we hunger for Him, the more we will want to read our Bibles, see the lost saved, fellowship with other believers, and to live holy even as He is holy (see I Peter 1:15-16).

If you are uncertain about what God is calling you to do, simply do what Tennent did: Ask Him to show you what gifts He gave you, and where you are to use them for His glory. If something in you wants to see **"the surpassing greatness of His power towards us who believe"** (**see Ephesians 1:19**), and you want to be continually **"filled with the Holy Spirit and . . . speak the word of God with boldness"** (**see Acts 4:31**), then pray as our forefathers prayed when they needed God to empower their powerless lives:

"...grant that Your bond-servants may speak Your word with all confidence,

while You extend Your hand to heal, and signs and wonders take place through the name of your holy servant Jesus" (Acts 4:29-30).

CONCLUSION

Truly it can be said of William Tennent that *"great teachers have little external history to record. Their lives go over into other lives."*[151] Although in the eyes of the world his life was not prominent, in the eyes of eternity it certainly was significant. But William and his students have long gone from us, and the Log College has long since turned to dust. So where does that leave us? And where does that leave God? He cannot use William Tennent anymore to start revival schools; nor can He use Gilbert Tennent or George Whitefield to awaken cities and regions. All He has to use is us—and for Him that is enough (see John 4:38). Like William Tennent, may you labor faithfully toward the vision God has placed in your heart.

The Log College monument on the old site of Tennent's homestead, where the school once stood. See also Appendix B. (Used by permission of the Spruance Library, Bucks County Historical Society.)

Appendix A
The Log of the Log College
(In order of graduation from school)

Student	Completed Schooling	Age at Graduation
Tennent, Gilbert	1724	1725-64
Tennent, John	1728	1729-33
Tennent, William, Jr.	1728	1731-77
Blair, Samuel	1733	1733-51
Alexander, David	1736	1736-41
Tennent, Charles	1736	1736-71
Rowland, John	1738	1738-47
McCrea, James	1739	1739-66
Bell, Hamilton	1739	1740-43
Robinson, William	1740	1740-46
Finley, Samuel	1740	1740-66
McKnight, Charles	1741	1741-78
Dean, William	1741	1742-48
Blair, John	1741	1741-71
Beatty, Charles	1742	1742-72
Roan, John	1742	1742-75
Redman, John	1742	Pre-1748-1808
Lawrence, Daniel	1744	1745-66
Smith, Robert	Pre-1747	Unknown
Campbell, John	1746	1747-53

Appendix A (continued)
The Log of the Log College
(In order of graduation from school)

Noted Accomplishments
Became a pastor and evangelist; trustee of College of New Jersey
Became a pastor.
Became a pastor; co-founder of a school (unknown); trustee of College of New Jersey.
Became a pastor; founder of Faggs Manor Academy; trustee of College of New Jersey.
Became a pastor.
Became a pastor.
Became a pastor and evangelist.
Referred to Log College by Charles Tennent; became a pastor.
Became a pastor and evangelist.
Former school teacher; converted by "Hellfire" Rowland; became a pastor and evangelist; involved in the "Hanover Revival."
Became a pastor; founder of West Nottingham Academy; trustee and president of College of New Jersey.
Became a pastor; co-founder of a school with William Tennent Jr.; captured during American Revolution; died soon after his release.
Former businessman; became a pastor.
Became a pastor; headmaster of Faggs Manor Academy; trustee and president-elect of College of New Jersey.
Former salesman; became William Tennent's successor at Neshaminy; trustee of College of New Jersey; missionary to Indians.
Grammar school teacher while studying at Log College; became a pastor.
Became a doctor; president of Philadelphia College of Physicians; trustee of Gilbert Tennent's church and College of New Jersey.
Became a pastor.
Became a pastor; founder of Pequea Academy; father of Samuel Smith (president of College of New Jersey).
Became a pastor.

Appendix B: The Lineage of the Log College

Inscribed on a monument to Tennent's Log College
are these words:

LUX IN TENEBRIS
LOG COLLEGE Organized By William Tennent, 1727

*Here, in the life of a pioneer teacher sound learning, endued with
spiritual passion, wrought to vitalize knowledge, glorify truth,
enrich life, and in due time call forth, to the glory of God and the
welfare of American youth, these worthy Christian colleges.*

1746	Princeton	1869	Wilson
1771	Queens	1872	Arkansas
1776	Hampton-Sydney	1875	Peark
1787	Washington & Jefferson	1875	Parsons
1794	Tusculum	1875	Southwestern
1812	Hamilton	1880	South Carolina
1819	Centre	1881	Coe
1819	Maryville	1882	Hastings
1826	Lafayette	1882	Emporia
1827	Hanover	1883	Huron
1827	Lindenwood	1883	Jamestown
1829	Illinois	1884	Grove City
1832	Wabash	1885	Macalester
1836	Davidson	1886	Alma
1842	Cumberland	1887	Occidental
1842	Mary Baldwin	1889	Daniel Baker
1846	Carroll	1889	Agnes Scott
1849	Westminster, Mo.	1889	Missouri Valley
1849	Austin	1890	Whitworth
1850	Waynesburg	1891	Buena Vista
1852	Dubuque	1891	College of Idaho
1853	Western	1891	College of Ozarks
1854	Lincoln University	1893	Belhaven
1855	Elmira	1894	Tulsa
1857	Blackburn	1895	Westminster, Utah
1857	Lake Forest	1896	Flora MacDonald
1863	Lincoln	1901	James Milliken
1866	Albany	1902	Texas Presbyterian
1866	Wooster	1904	Davis & Elkins
1867	King	1906	Chicora
1867	Johnson & Smith	1923	Intermountain
1869	Trinity		

ENDNOTES

CHAPTER ONE

[1]*Doylestown Daily Intelligencer,* (Vol. IV, No.1) "The Log College," Doylestown, PA: September 6, 1889.

[2]Booth, Anna. Quote by Yeats, *Not the Filling of a Pail, But the Lighting of a Fire,* (www.public.asu.edu/~aestarr/documents/educational_platform.pdf) p. 1.

[3]Strong, James. *Strong's Exhaustive Concordance.* TN: Dugan Publishers, Inc. *Greek Dictionary of the New Testament,* #2821, p. 42.

[4]Lowman, Michael. *United States History in Christian Perspective.* Pensacola, FL: A Beka Book Publications, 1982, p. 67.

[5]*"Doylestown Daily Intelligencer."*

[6]Mumford, Bob, *About Bob & Judith Mumford* (www.lifechangers.com/html2/about_bob.php)

CHAPTER TWO

[7]Klett, Guy S. *Minutes of the Presbyterian Church in America (1706-1788).* Philadelphia, PA: Presbyterian Historical Society, 1976, p. 211.

[8]Thompson, George. *World History and Cultures in Christian Perspective.* A Beka Book: Pensacola, FL 1986, p. 221.

[9]Barkley, John M. *The Presbyterian Church in Ireland, Part I.* Journal of Presbyterian History. Vol. #44 (Dec. 1966), p. 258-59. For a well-researched history on William Tennent's early life, see *A History of Neshaminy-Warwick Presbyterian Church 1726-1976,* by Helen H. Gemmill (Nash Printing, Lansdale, PA: 1976).

[10]Schnittjer, Gary E. *William Tennent and the Log College.* (Master's Thesis for Dallas Theological Seminary), 1992, p. 39-51.

[11]Ibid, p. 55.

CHAPTER THREE

[12]Klett, p. 34.

[13]From Tennent's personal journal called "Hicse Libellus," p. 20. (Cited in Tennent, Mary A. *Light In Darkness,* Greensboro, NC: Greensboro Printing Co., 1971, p. 30.)

[14]Klett, p. 34.

[15]Ibid.

[16]Tennent, M. p. 31-32.

[17]Pears, Jr., Thomas C. and Klett, Guy S. *Documentary History of William Tennent and the Log College*. Philadelphia: Presbyterian Historical Society, 1940, p. 23.

[18]Dexter, Franklin Bowditch. *Yale Biographies and Annals*. (Cited in Tennent, M. p. 72.)

[19]Schnittjer, p. 23.

[20]From a letter to the congregation in Piles Grove, stored at the Presbyterian Historical Society (Philadelphia). (Cited in Schnittjer, p. 26.)

[21]Pears and Klett, p. 164.

[22]Peabody, Larry. *Secular Work Is Full-Time Service*. Ft. Washington, PA: Christian Literature Crusade, 1974, p. 19.

[23]Pears and Klett, p. 32, 35.

[24]"Neshaminy" is of the Lenni Lenape tribe's Algonquin language. (MacReynolds, George. *Place Names of Bucks County*. Doylestown: The Bucks County Historical Society, 1942, p.1.)

CHAPTER FOUR

[25]Bushman, Richard L. *The Great Awakening: Documents on the Revival of Religion (1740-1745)*. New York: Institute of Early American History & Culture at Williamsburg, VA, 1970, p. 9.

[26]Whitefield, George. *George Whitefield's Journals*. Carlisle, PA: The Banner of Truth Trust, 1998, p. 352.

[27]Messler, Abraham. *Forty Years at Raritan*. New York: A. Lloyd, 1873. (Cited in Beeke, Joel R. *Theodorus Jacobus Frelinghuysen (1691-1747): Precursor of the Great Awakening*, The Banner of Truth (Issue #407-8) Edinburgh: Banner Of Truth Trust, 1997, p.40.)

[28]Beeke, p. 40, 42.

[29]Ibid, p.43-44.

[30]Coalter, Milton J. *Gilbert Tennent, Son of Thunder*. New York: Greenwood Press, 1986, p.22.

[31]Beeke, p. 45.

[32]Sweet, William. *Revivalism in America*. New York: Charles Scribner's Sons, 1944, p.53.

[33]Gillies, John. *Historical Collections of Accounts of Revivals*. Carlisle, PA: Banner of Truth Trust, 1981, p. vii.

[34]Henry, Matthew. *Matthew Henry's Commentary on the Whole Bible, (Vol. V)*. Hendrickson Publishers, Inc. 1996, Vol. V, p. 703.

[35]Gillies, p. vii.

[36]Tennent, Gilbert. *A Solemn Warning to the Secure World*, Boston: S. Kneeland and T. Green, 1735, p. ii.

[37]Ibid, p.v, vii.

[38]Boudinot, Elias C. *Life of the Reverend William Tennent*. Hartford: S. Andrus & Son, 1845, p. 29-31. See also p. 109-111.

[39]Tennent, G. *A Solemn Warning*. p. xi-xii.

[40]From William Tennent Sr.'s sermon, *No Man Can Come To Me Unless The Father Draw Him...* (Cited in Schnittjer, p. 111.)

CHAPTER FIVE

[41]Booth, p. 1.

[42]Tennent, G. *The Danger of an Unconverted Ministry, 1740*. (Cited in Alexander, Archibald *Sermons of the Log College*. Ligonier, PA: Soli Deo Gloria Publications, 1993, p. 378, 380.)

[43]Tennent, G. *A Solemn Warning*, p. xiii.

[44]Increase Mather (1639-1723). (Hodge, Charles. *The Constitutional History of the Presbyterian Church in the United States of America*. Philadelphia, PA: Presbyterian Board of Publication, 1851, Part II, p. 17.)

[45]Whitefield, *Journals*, p. 470.

[46]Thomson John. *An Overture Presented to the Reverend Synod of Dissenting Ministers...* September, 1728. Philadelphia: Samuel Keimer, 1729, p. 30.

[47]William's son Charles described the College as *"near twenty feet long, and almost ten feet wide."* *A Second Letter to the Congregation of the Eighteen Presbyterian Ministers...* Philadelphia: A. Steuart, 1761. (Cited in Pears, p. 163.) George Whitefield, however, believed it to be twenty feet by twenty feet. (Whitefield, *Journals*, p. 354.)

[48]Whitefield, *Journals*. p. 354.

[49]Smith, Robert. *The Detection Detected, Or A Vindication Of The Rev. Mr. Delap, and New Castle Presbytery...*, 1757, p. 124. (Cited in Trinterud, Leonard. *The Forming of an American Tradition: A Re-examination of Colonial Presbyterianism*. Philadelphia, PA: The Westminster Press, 1949, p. 327.)

[50]Booth, p.1.

[51]Tennent, Gilbert. *The Examiner Examined, or Gilbert Tennent, Harmonious.* Philadelphia: William Bradford, 1743, p. 96.

[52]From W. Tennent Sr.'s sermon, "No Man Can Come.." (Cited in Schnittjer, p. 111.)

[53]Henry, p. 583; Oliphant, Hugh. "Gilbert Tennent and the Preaching of Piety in Colonial America: Newly Discovered Manuscripts in Speer Library." *The Princeton Seminary Bulletin (Vol. 10, #2).* Princeton: Princeton Theological Seminary, 1989, p. 136.

[54]From W. Tennent's sermon, "No Man Can Come..." (Cited in Schnittjer, p. 113.).

[55]Tennent, G. "A Letter to Stephen Williams," not dated. Stored at the Presbyterian Historical Society. (Cited in Schnittjer, p. 222.)

[56]From Edwards' sermon, "A Spiritual Understanding of Divine Things..." (Cited from *The Works Of Jonathan Edwards (Vol. 14)* New Haven: Yale University, 1997, p. 67-68, 76-77.)

[57]Pears and Klett, p. 93-94.

[58]Pears and Klett, p. 95.

[59]Ibid, p. 96.

[60]Klett, *Minutes.* p.142.

[61]Pears and Klett, p. 96.

[62]Klett, *Minutes,* p. 148-49.

[63]Ibid, p. 157.

[64]Ibid, p. 160.

[65]Ibid, p. 166.

CHAPTER SEVEN

[66]en.thinkexist.com/quotes/francis_scott_fitzgerald/

[67]Klett, *Minutes,* p. 157.

[68]Tennent, G. "The Legal Bow..." (1739), p.17. (Cited in Trinterud, p. 57.)

[69]Henry, Vol. V, p. 753.

[70]Klett, *Minutes,* p. 211.

[71]Ibid.

[72]Ibid. See also Gillespie, George. *A Sermon Against Divisions in the Churches.* Philadelphia: William Bradford, 1740, p. viii.

[73]*New Brunswick Presbytery, Minutes 1738-1756, Vol. I, August 8, 1738.* Philadelphia: Presbyterian Historical Society. See also Coalter, p. 51.

[74]Alison, Francis. *An Examination and Refutation of Mr. Gilbert Tennent's Remarks Upon the Protestation Presented to the Synod of Philadelphia, June 1, 1741*. Philadelphia: Ben Franklin, 1742, p. 21.

[75]"Minutes of Philadelphia Presbytery, Philadelphia Historical Society, Sept. 19, 1738." (Cited in Coalter, p. 51.)

[76]"New Brunswick Presbytery's Disregard of Acts of Synod" (Cited in Coalter, p. 51.)

[77]Pears and Klett, p. 109.

[78]Klett, *Minutes*, p. 162.

[79]Ibid, p. 164.

[80]Ibid, p. 165, 211.

[81]Ibid, p. 212.

[82]Pears and Klett, p. 114-115.

CHAPTER EIGHT

[83]Edwards, Jonathan. *A Faithful Narrative of the Surprising Work of God*. (www.iclnet.org/pub/resources/text/ipb-e/epl-10/web/edwards-narrative.html)

[84]Whitefield, *Journals*, p. 46.

[85]Ibid, p.47.

[86]Ibid, p. 46.

[87]Ibid, p. 58.

[88]Dallimore, Arnold. *George Whitefield: The Life and Times of the Great Evangelist of the 18th Century Revival (Vol.1)*. Carlisle, PA: The Banner Of Truth Trust, 1989, p. 400.

[89]Sweet, *Revivalism*, p. 108.

[90]Whitefield, *Journals*, p. 344-45, 347.

[91]Ibid, p. 347-48.

[92]Dickinson, Jonathan. *Danger of Schisms and Contentions with Respect to the Ministry and Ordinances of the Gospel*. New York: Zenger, 1739, p. 9-10, 21.

[93]Whitefield, *Journals*, p. 351.

[94]Ibid, p. 351, 353.

[95]Ibid, p. 354-55.

[96]Whitefield, George. *George Whitefield's Letters (1734 to 1742)*. Carlisle, PA: The Banner of Truth Trust, 1976, p. 144.

[97]Pears, Thomas C. "Colonial Education Among Presbyterians," *The Journal of Presbyterian History* (Vol. 76, No.1—Spring, 1998), p. 22.

[98]Whitefield, George. *Three Letters to the Reverend Mr. George Whitefield.* Philadelphia: Andrew Bradford, 1739, p. 8-12.

[99]Dallimore, p. 400.

[100]McCormick, Richard. *Rutgers: A Bicentennial History.* New Brunswick, NJ: Rutgers University Press, 1966, p. 3.

[101]Tennent, G. *The Examiner Examined.* p. 96.

CHAPTER NINE

[102]Alexander, *Sermons*, p. 397.

[103]*The Pennsylvania Gazette,* April 6, 1758 (June 12, 1740 edition) (#21649).

[104]Franklin, Benjamin. *The Autobiography of Benjamin Franklin.* New York: Collier Books, 1962, p. 101,103.

[105]Prince, Thomas. *The Christian History.* Boston: 1745, 2:385. (Cited in Gillies, p. xii.)

[106]Henry, Vol. V, p. 707.

[107]Alexander, *Sermons*, p. 381-2, 384, 386, 388-9, 391, 393-4, 397.

[108]Ingraham, George. "History of the Presbytery of New Brunswick, Pt. III," *Journal of the Presbyterian Historical Society 7 (Sept., 1913)*, p. 150. (Cited in Schnittjer, p. 199.)

[109]Seward, p. 12. (Cited in Schnittjer, p. 198-9.) Whitefield, *Letters.* p. 145.

[110]Pears and Klett, p. 125.

[111]Hancock, John. *The Examiner, or Gilbert Against Tennent.* Philadelphia: William Bradford: 1743, p 18.

[112]Tennent, G. *The Examiner Examined.* p. 94-96.

[113]Tennent, Gilbert. *Remarks Upon a Protestation...*Philadelphia: W. Dunlap, 1760, p. 9.

[114]Hodge, p. 150,154.

CHAPTER TEN

[115]Leitch, Alexander. *A Princeton Companion.* Princeton, NJ: Princeton University Press, 1978, p. 199.

[116]Pears and Klett, p. 142.

[117]*Mss. Records of the New Brunswick Presbytery* p. 39. (Cited in Pears and Klett, p. 132.)

[118]Irwin, Nathaniel. *Memoirs of the Neshaminy Church, 1793.* (Cited in Pears and Klett, p. 166-67.)

[119]Alexander, Archibald. *Biographical Sketches of the Founder and Principal Alumni of the Log College.* Philadelphia, PA: Presbyterian Board of Publication, 1851, p. 23, 50.

[120]Leitch, p. 199.

[121]Spoken by one of the Trustees. (Leitch, p. 199.)

[122]*New York Gazette,* Feb. 2, 1747 edition. (Trinterud, p. 125.)

[123]*Indenture for the New Building,* November 14, 1740. (Coalter, p. 108.)

[124]Eavey, C.B. *History of Christian Education.* Chicago: Moody Press, 1964, p. 200.

[125]Leitch, p. 134; Klett, *Minutes,* p. 165-66.

[126]Samuel Davies and Gilbert Tennent. *A General Account of the Rise and State of the College...(1754).* (Cited in The American Colonist's Library: A Treasury 0f Primary Documents, www.personal.pitnet.net/primarysources/princeton.html)

[127]Henry, Vol. 5, p. 707.

[128]Tennent, Gilbert. *A Persuasive to the Right Use of the Passions in Religion.* Philadelphia: W. Dunlap, 1760, p. 1.

[129]Tennent, Gilbert. *Irenicum Ecclesiasticum, Or a Humble Impartial Essay Upon the Peace of Jerusalem.* Philadelphia: William Bradford, 1749, p. iv-vi.

[130]Whitefield, *Journals,* p. 354. For the Princeton connection, see also Trinterud, p.125 and Selden, William K. *Princeton Theological Seminary: A Narrative History (1812-1992).* Princeton: Princeton University Press, 1992, p. 6.

CHAPTER ELEVEN

[131]Firestone, Harvey S. www.brainyquote.com/quotes/quotes/h/harveysfi158287.html

[132]*The Pennsylvania Gazette,* April 6, 1758. #21649

[133]Leitch, p. 127.

[134]Ibid, p. 126; Sloan, Douglas. *The Scottish Enlightenment and the American College Idea.* VT: Teachers Press College, 1971, p. 50.

[135]Miller, Glenn. *Religious Liberty in America.* Philadelphia: Westminster Press, 1976, p. 57-58.

[136]Niebuhr, H. Richard. *The Ministry in Historical Perspective.* San Francisco: Harper and Row, 1983, p. 242.

[137]Sermon by Samuel Willard in 1700. (Bushman, p. 9.)

[138]Foote, William Henry. *Sketches of North Carolina, Historical and Biographical, Illustrative of the Principles of a Portion of Her Early Settlers.* New York: 1846, p. 235.

[139]Caldwell, David Andrew. *David Caldwell, 1725-1824.* California: DAC Press, 2000, p. 15.

[140]Alexander, *Biographical.* p. 12.

[141]*The Princeton Seminary Catalogue (Vol. XXVII, No. 1, July 2003).* Princeton, NJ: Princeton Theological Seminary, p. 31-32.

[142]Eidsmoe, John. *God and Caesar.* Westchester, IL: Crossway Books, 1984, p. 151; McNergney, Robert. *Foundations of Education.* Boston: Allyn and Bacon, 2001, p. 64.

[143]Barton, David. "Unconfirmed Quotes," *Wallbuilders.* (www.wallbuilders.com/)

[144]Luther, Martin. "To the Christian Nobility of the German Nation Concerning the Reform of the Christian Estate, 1520." (Atkinson, James. *Luther's Works: The Christian in Society II* (Vol. 44). Augsburg Fortress Publishers, 1966, p. 207.)

CHAPTER TWELVE

[145]Wallis, Arthur. *In the Day of Thy Power.* Fort Washington, PA: Christian Literature Crusade, 1990, p. 249.

[146]Calian, Carnegie. *The Ideal Seminary.* Louisville: Westminster John Knox Press, 2002, p. xii.

[147]Chacha, Dr. John N. *Teamwork Bible College International, 2002-03 Administrative Manual and Catalog,* p. 5.

[148]Tillapaugh, Frank R. *Unleashing the Church: Getting People Out of the Fortress and Into Ministry.* Ventura, CA: Regal Books, 1982, p. 134-5.

[149]Tillapaugh, p. 131.

[150]"The Wit and Wisdom of Albert Einstein." (www.freaky_freya.tripod.com/einstein.html)

[151]Script line from Universal Studios movie *The Emperor's Club,* (See "The Story," www.theemperorsclub.com)